ROUTLEDGE LIBRARY EDITIONS:
POLITICAL THOUGHT AND
POLITICAL PHILOSOPHY

Volume 28

NIKOLAI BUKHARIN AND THE TRANSITION FROM CAPITALISM TO SOCIALISM

NIKOLAI BUKHARIN AND THE TRANSITION FROM CAPITALISM TO SOCIALISM

MICHAEL HAYNES

Routledge
Taylor & Francis Group

LONDON AND NEW YORK

First published in 1985 by Croom Helm Ltd

This edition first published in 2020
by Routledge
2 Park Square, Milton Park, Abingdon, Oxon OX14 4RN

and by Routledge
52 Vanderbilt Avenue, New York, NY 10017

Routledge is an imprint of the Taylor & Francis Group, an informa business

British Library Cataloguing in Publication Data
A catalogue record for this book is available from the British Library

ISBN: 978-0-367-21961-1 (Set)
ISBN: 978-0-429-35434-2 (Set) (ebk)
ISBN: 978-0-367-24436-1 (Volume 28) (hbk)
ISBN: 978-0-367-24439-2 (Volume 28) (pbk)
ISBN: 978-0-429-28240-9 (Volume 28) (ebk)

Publisher's Note
The publisher has gone to great lengths to ensure the quality of this reprint but points out that some imperfections in the original copies may be apparent.

Disclaimer
The publisher has made every effort to trace copyright holders and would welcome correspondence from those they have been unable to trace.

NIKOLAI BUKHARIN & THE TRANSITION FROM CAPITALISM TO SOCIALISM

MICHAEL HAYNES

CROOM HELM
London & Sydney

©1985 Michael Haynes
Croom Helm Ltd, Provident House, Burrell Row,
Beckenham, Kent BR3 1AT
Croom Helm Australia Pty Ltd, First Floor,
139 King Street, Sydney, NSW 2001, Australia

British Library Cataloguing in Publication Data

Haynes, Michael
    Nikolai Bukharin and the transition from
    capitalism to socialism.
    1. Bukharin, N. 2. Socialism — Soviet Union
    — History — 20th century
    I. Title   HX313
    335'.0092'4

    ISBN 0-7099-3740-7

Typeset by Columns of Reading
Printed and bound in Great Britain
by Billing & Sons Limited, Worcester.

CONTENTS

For Marcie, Rachel and Matthew

PREFACE

Prefaces should be brief and workmanlike. As far as possible I have given references to the many English and French translations that exist of Bukharin's writings. Obscure and poor though these sometimes are I have done this in the belief that they will be more accessible to the majority of readers (as they were to me) than references to the original Russian. For anyone who wishes to consult the originals it is a relatively simple matter to trace them through Sidney Heitman's invaluable bibliography of Bukharin's writings, *Nikolai I. Bukharin: A Bibliography*, Stanford: Hoover Institution, 1969. Where I have used these translations I have occasionally taken the liberty of trying to clarify some of them. All emphases (which are common in Russian) are those of the authors quoted unless otherwise stated.

For various reasons this book has been a long time coming and some acknowledgement of help received is now much overdue. My most recent debt is to Richard Stoneman at Croom Helm whose commendable speed in dealing with the manuscript puts others to shame. Tracing some of the more obscure of Bukharin's writings has only been possible because of the resources and help of particular libraries. In particular I owe a debt to the Alexander Baykov Library at the University of Birmingham, the British Library of Political and Economic Science and the library at Wolverhampton Polytechnic (and especially John Nockles). Support from the Polytechnic, Wolverhampton, also enabled me to draw on the resources of the Institute of Social History in Amsterdam and various libraries in Paris, especially the Bibliothèque de documentation internationale contemporaine at Nanterre, and the Institut Maurice Thorez.

My stay in Paris was made all the more pleasant by contacts with, and help from, Maurice Andreau, Wladimir Andreff, Bernard Chavance and Christian Salmon. Similarly in Amsterdam Kees van der Pijl went out of his way to make me welcome. At home Peter Binns, Bruce Young and Marcie Haynes have all laboured to improve the manuscript in its various versions. My colleague Dr Neil Malcolm has proved an ever patient guide when my knowledge of Russian has proved inadequate. Needless to say these acknowledgements in no way imply agreement with what follows and all defects, whether of translation, argument or whatever I lay claim to myself.

Michael Haynes

1 INTRODUCTION

Writing in the mid-nineteenth century the French revolutionary, Auguste Blanqui, likened revolution to crossing a river. Instead of standing on the bank quarrelling over whether the field on the other side was wheat or rye, he wrote, the point is to cross and see! In this, at least, Marx too would have been at one with Blanqui's impatience. He also had little time for those for whom socialism consisted of idle speculation about the blueprints for some ideal society. It was Marx's strength, as Lenin later stressed, that he had no truck with such utopianism. On the contrary, Marx's early work had been a struggle against the proponents of 'new moral worlds' and for a recognition of the working class as the class which would make socialism through its own conscious action. Yet by Lenin's time the inadequacy of this, except as a most preliminary answer to the question of the nature of the transition to socialism, was already becoming apparent. Indeed, Lenin himself then went on to write *State and Revolution*, a book which does nothing if not dispute the nature of the field on the other side of the river. Moreover, he wrote this in the very midst of the Russian Revolution – clearly it was not sufficient just to cross the river and see.

What then had changed? What led Lenin and the Bolsheviks, even before the October Revolution had successfully overthrown the Tsarist state, to spend so much energy considering the nature of the transition to socialism? And what makes it important to take up this question again today? Certainly the answer does not lie in some new-found respect for the utopian socialists of old. It lies rather in the recognition that the problem of how to cross the river (and here Blanqui's analogy breaks down) cannot be separated from the question of whether the field on the other side is really of wheat or rye. In short, the issue of the transition to socialism takes us directly to the heart of contemporary debates about capitalism and the possibility of socialism.

Lenin was writing against a background of discussion in the Second International in which the problem of the transition to socialism had received little explicit attention. Socialism increasingly appeared as a distant utopia which related to the present only as an abstract moral goal. The leading social-democrats of the day came, in practice, to adopt a position that has been likened to that of the Victorian clergyman who assured his doubting parishioner that the Second Coming

1

was undoubtedly on its way — but hopefully it would not arrive in their lifetime. In this way the whole question came to have an air of unreality which was well summed up by the French communist Alfred Rosmer, 'when the issue had come up as an obstacle in discussion it had been evaded. The transition had been seen as a leap from capitalist society into an ideal society to be constructed at leisure . . . this was the realm of fairy-tales.'[1]

This failure to confront the problem of the transition to socialism had important consequences in the Second International. It was a central part of the separation of means from ends that came to characterise the politics of the social-democratic parties before the first world war. Their programmes were divided into sets of maximum and minimum demands, but increasingly the links between the two became more tenuous. This shift was common to the whole of the Second International and the story of how it contributed to the break-up of the International in the face of war in August 1914 is well known. What is less often appreciated is the negative impact it also had on the development of Marxist theory. On the face of it, the giants of the Second International like Karl Kautsky, Rudolph Hilferding, Otto Bauer and others all pushed Marxism forward in new directions but, when the Bolsheviks rejected the politics of the Second International they also rejected much of its theoretical underpinnings as well. In important respects they challenged the accepted canons on such central questions as the state, imperialism, and the world economy. In this sense the break that had occurred in the Second International between the analysis of capitalism and the analysis of the transition to socialism displaced both politics and theory.

Today the background is, of course, very different from that of the era of the Russian Revolution, but it is this that makes a re-examination of the question of capitalism and the transition to socialism more urgent. Capitalism has changed enormously since the early years of this century. Over the past three decades it has experienced the greatest surge of accumulation in its history. Its structures have been transformed as capital has grown, merged and concentrated. The state is now an ever-present actor directly assisting in accumulation; and yet, at another level, capital seems to transcend national forms as huge multinational companies compete in the world market where they dwarf even medium-sized states. Is this still a capitalism we can recognise? If the optimistic hopes of a 'post-capitalist' society now seem shallow so too do those attempts on the Left to pretend that it is 'all in Marx'.

At the core of the world economy the strength of the system was sapped in the 1970s. 'Fine tuning' the domestic economies of the advanced world has been shown to be insufficient to balance unemployment and inflation. The business-cycle is far from obsolete, and we can now dispense with the euphemism of *recession* and talk openly of *depression*. But, for all this, the system has not crashed on the scale or in the manner that it did between 1929 and 1933. Can the crisis be managed? Many on the Left would seem to suggest that it can. As faith in post-war Keynesianism has given way to a much less self-confident post-Keynesian economics and a hostile monetarism, so the Left has rediscovered the 'original' radical soul of Keynes to justify national roads to recovery in the first instance, and then socialism in the long run. Industry can be wrested from the hands of private capital and regenerated by the state, protected from the chill winds of the world economy by a temporary wall of trade barriers.

Nor is this type of solution unique to the advanced world. In the so-called Third World three decades of unparalleled boom in the world economy have been sufficient to lift only a few of the poorer economies from the pit of economic backwardness. For the rest the dictates of the world economy have continued to enforce a basic dependency as raw material producers. Does the solution then lie in destroying this dependency and breaking free of the world economy? Is this the path that the mass of humanity must take in their transition to socialism? That it is has been a central part of much radical thinking about development over the past decade. Attractive to, if not sponsored by, professional and state élites in these societies such policies of national independence find wider and wider support as the already inadequate stimulus from the advanced world weakens.

But what then of that part of the world which claims to have already established some form of socialism? How are we to understand their experience as their problems force them into an ever closer dependency on the world economy? States as diverse as the Soviet Union, Yugoslavia, China, Tanzania, Libya all claim to have established at least the rudiments of socialism though they cannot agree on what these are, and if they have problems in this respect then so too do we as they also lurch into crises which seem no less deep than those of the West. Have they really broken with capitalism? Can we identify a different set of social processes operating in them? Is the rhythm of their systems and of revolt against them really that different from the rhythm in the West? If they are a picture of the future, if only at the level of economic organisation — why do they not work?

It is against a background of debate on issues like these that this book has been written. It tries to break through the compartmentalisation of these problems and to raise general questions about the nature of capitalism and the transition to socialism. It does so through a critical study of the contribution made to this question by the Russian Marxist, Nikolai Bukharin. Our argument will be twofold. First, that Bukharin was the one twentieth-century Marxist to provide the basis for a coherent analysis of capitalism and the transition to socialism which still stands the test of time. Secondly, we shall argue that in important respects Bukharin's analysis is still in advance of much contemporary discussion, and to the extent that it can be reappropriated it can advance that discussion. In this latter sense, our purpose is significantly more than that of writing an intellectual history which traces the antecedents of accepted positions since the positions themselves are still controversial.

These are large claims to make for Bukharin, and the reader must judge at the end of the book whether they have been sustained. But one of the reasons that they may sound more grandiose than they should is that the legacy of Bukharin's work has been subject to the vicissitudes of historical reinterpretation in such a way as to obscure much of his real theoretical contribution. In this respect the calumnies visited on Bukharin in the 1930s by Stalin's propagandists are *relatively* easy to lift, but the situation is more complex with the recent reassessment of Bukharin's career and politics. Since we shall differ from this reassessment on a whole number of points it may be helpful to offer the reader some guideposts to what is at stake and how the discussion that follows will differ from the previous debates.

Over the past two decades a major academic battle has been fought out in the West over Bukharin's political legacy, a debate given further point by a renewed interest in some of his ideas amongst reformers in Eastern Europe and the brief flowering of a campaign for his political rehabilitation in the Soviet Union.[2] Grouped on one side in this clash we find the orthodox historians of Soviet Russia who have been heavily influenced in their analysis by parts of Trotsky's argument though not by his politics. On the other side is a liberal revisionist school led by Bukharin's biographer, Stephen Cohen. What has really been at issue between the two sides is less Bukharin than the interpretation of Soviet history and the rise of Stalin. Bukharin, however, has been the site of the battle. For the former school Trotsky's arguments on the rise of Stalin have been used to argue fatalistically for its necessity. Given the failure of the utopian hopes of permanent revolution, the rise of Stalin was an inevitable consequence of the degeneration of the Russian

Revolution: regrettable and unfortunate perhaps, but without doubt necessary. For the revisionists there is no such necessity. Stalin could have been opposed and was opposed by a liberal alternative which, whilst also rejecting the romantic hopes of world revolution, did offer a real alternative to the totalitarian regime that Russia became in the 1930s. If this opposition failed it was not because it conflicted with some inevitable logic of industrial*ism* or totalitarian*ism* or any other *ism* but because of real historical factors. In this way an historical alternative is opened up. It did not have to happen this way. And at the centre of this alternative is Nikolai Bukharin. He was defeated by Stalin in 1928 and 1929, but what was truly inevitable about this?

The debate has ranged far and wide and it has thrown up many fascinating contributions including Cohen's major historical biography. Whether it has done full justice to Bukharin and his Marxism is less clear because his Marxism has not been the issue – indeed, it has often seemed a positive embarrassment to many of the participants. Not only have they reduced Bukharin's contribution to the development of Marxism to specifically Russian dimensions (so losing sight of his intention to analyse capitalism as a whole), but they have then shrunk his arguments to fit alternative models of Soviet history whose assumptions he may not have accepted and would at least have found problematic.

In this respect the traditional orthodoxy in whatever form finds least difficulty with Bukharin. He stands condemned for his apparent political instability in Russian politics in the 1920s. In this account, taking its cue from Trotsky (who is often imbibed indirectly through the histories of Isaac Deutscher and E.H. Carr), Bukharin is pictured as the wayward theorist who paved the way for Stalin's rise to power. Having joined the Bolshevik Party after the revolution of 1905 he distinguished himself until 1921 as a representative of the Left. Then, turning to the 'Right' under the influence of the New Economic Policy with its more positive evaluation of the role of the peasantry, he opposed Trotsky and worked hand-in-glove with Stalin to defeat the Left opposition. Not until 1928 and 1929 did he realise the dangers in his support for Stalin. Then on the eve of industrialisation he drew back, but his subsequent opposition was too little and too late to save him. His eventual death as a result of the third and greatest purge trial in 1938 was rough justice no doubt, but justice nevertheless for the ambiguous role he had played. If Bukharin has any attraction then, according to this interpretation, it is only that of an innocent who acted in good faith in a world too big for him.

Interestingly, the revisionists accept much of this interpretation.

Against it historians like Stephen Cohen and Moshe Lewin have tried to vindicate Bukharin by arguing that between 1926 and 1927 he redefined his policies to create the basis for a genuine alternative to the policies supported by Stalin. It is in this later guise that Bukharin assumes a decisive significance, and his earlier role is then reinterpreted to fit this perspective. As a result there tends to be as much dismissal of his Marxism as a whole as there is in the orthodox case.[3]

What is important for us is to recognise the narrowness of the focus of this whole discussion and the way in which both sides dismiss and disparage Bukharin's Marxism. For the revisionists what is important is the defence of a particular set of policies. If these clash with earlier positions held by Bukharin then so much the worse for these earlier positions: they can be written off as romantic and youthful excesses compared to his later realism. For Bukharin's opponents there are no such problems, the contradictions in his position need not be analysed, they can be dismissed as part of the weaknesses which led to his general failure. Though not immune himself to the occasional piece of middle-aged romanticism, like his continued support of international revolution, Trotsky was right in his 1920s' critique of Bukharin, and if Trotsky's argument leads to ambiguities over the assessment of Stalin's industrialisation this is so much the better. These very ambiguities in Trotsky enable him to be drawn on all the more widely. And in all this Bukharin lays claim to our attention only for his role in Soviet history and not as a central figure in the development of Marxism after Marx.

In contrast, our concern will be with Bukharin the Marxist. His analysis is our central interest and from this basis it becomes possible to redefine the issues fought over in the recent debates and to get both a better understanding of Bukharin's real contribution as well as an awareness of its real limitations. Starting with his discussion of capitalism, we shall explore his political economy as a whole, identifying and working out the contradictions in the positions at which he arrived. Our analysis will not be uncritical. At a number of points we shall suggest different conclusions from those which he eventually drew. But, unlike other accounts, if we disagree with the path he took it will be because we draw different conclusions from his premises — not because we are working from a different position. Moreover, this said, we shall then argue for the power and the vision of his general analysis. Without a development of his arguments, albeit a critical one, the modern world cannot be understood.

Notes

1. A. Rosmer, *Lenin's Moscow*, London: Pluto Press, 1971, p. 60.
2. See K. Coates, *The Case of Nikolai Bukharin*, Nottingham: Spokesman, 1978.
3. S. Cohen, *Bukharin and the Bolshevik Revolution*, Oxford: Oxford University Press, 1980, *passim*; M. Lewin, *Political Undercurrents in Soviet Economic Debates*, London: Pluto Press, 1974, *passim*.

2 CAPITALISM AS A WORLD ECONOMY

Nikolai Bukharin was born in 1889 at a time when the tide of imperial expansion was in full flood. Often supported on the ground only by adventurers and missionaries, the European powers raced to secure their place in the sun. By the time of Bukharin's adolescence the map of the world had effectively been painted in European colours. In the three and a half decades before the first world war, territory was colonised at an average rate of some quarter of a million square miles each year. Europe had divided the world, and as it did so the world became divided by the divisions in Europe. Then, in August 1914 the whole system seemed to recoil, the expansion of European capitalism turned in on itself. Europe's war became a world war but the struggle for world power now took place in the mud of a not so distant field. For four years the immediate contest was to gain or defend a few thousand yards – at times a few hundred yards – of European territory and for this at Ypres, Verdun, the Somme, Passchendaele more men were sacrificed each day than had been lost in conquering tens of thousands of square miles in Africa and Asia.

In trying to relate to these dramatic events Marxists obviously attempted to build on the body of Marx's then published work. But they were immediately confronted with two difficulties. The first was that important parts of Marx's analysis were incomplete and on some accounts fatally flawed. Here there was scope for a long line of controversies on value theory, reproduction and crisis which periodically rent the social-democratic movement as new 'solutions' to real and imagined problems were regularly produced. In this tradition at the time of the first world war Marxists were busy rebutting Rosa Luxemburg's radical challenge to orthodoxy in her book *The Accumulation of Capital*. There she claimed to have shown that capitalism could only exist as a dynamic force so long as surplus value produced in the heart of the system could be realised in non-capitalist third markets. Once these non-capitalist markets had been conquered and integrated into capitalism then the system must inevitably enter into decline, facing the world with the choice of 'socialism or barbarism'.

Debates in this and related areas still continue to divide Marxists and their history is well documented.[1] But there was and is a second level of difficulty with Marx's work which has no less significance for the analysis of capitalism but which was less sharply perceived at the time. In the first volume of *Capital* Marx's method was to analyse what he called 'capital in general'; that is, not capitalism as it actually existed but the essence of capital. To do this he analysed either the way in which capital in total functions or capitalism as a closed and developed system ignoring, for the moment, that capitalism actually exists in a world of many competing capitals. As he himself noted in a footnote to which Rosa Luxemburg drew attention,

> in order to examine the object of our investigation in its integrity, free from all disturbing subsidiary circumstances, we must treat the whole world of trade as one nation, and assume that capitalist production is established everywhere and has taken possession of every branch of industry.[2]

Marx, then, intended to remove this abstraction from the real world of competitive relations and in subsequent volumes to work up through the various layers between theory and the real world. The plan of *Capital* includes volumes on the state, international trade and the world market and crises. At the time of his death he had barely scratched the surface of these topics and it has only been in more recent years that the fuller logic of his analysis has been reconstructed.[3] Marxists before the first world war then, had to do this job themselves if they were to confront Marx's analysis with the increasingly complex world of capitalism. But how was this to be done? With hindsight we can see that two alternative answers developed within the Second International.

By far the most influential analysis was that which saw capitalism as a series of national forms. Marx's analysis of 'capital in general' was identified with British or German or French capitalisms with the competition of many capitals taking place within the national boundaries. Each of these national forms had its own dynamic of development which led through primitive communism to slavery, feudalism, capitalism and the eventual triumph of socialism. The central political distinction that followed from this was between those countries which had already experienced a bourgeois revolution and those which had not. Only in the former could the working class have any expectation of taking power. Elsewhere, although it might be forced to play a leading role in particular situations, it had to wait for the long-term development of its 'historical mission'. The fact that the world was made up of many different 'national capitals' did not present any serious theoretical problem. The interaction between them was interpreted as a spilling-over of what were identified as internal developments into the external sphere. Inevitably this led to problems, even to war, but it did not modify the national character of the system. In its most sophisticated form this was the analysis put forward by Rudolf Hilferding in his famous book *Finance Capital* published in 1910. The fact that Hilferding was one of the first Marxists to analyse imperialism at all has tended to obscure the way in which his analysis comes almost as an afterthought to his discussion of the centralisation of capital in the national form.

This analysis was also taken up by Karl Kautsky in his discussion of capitalism and imperialism, and it led him to write his famous article on 'Ultra-Imperialism', completed a few weeks before the outbreak of the first world war. Here he suggested that the different national capitalisms might come to see it as in their own interests to form 'a holy alliance of the imperialists' which would divide the world peaceably as 'a federation of the strongest who renounce their arms race'. In this way the cartelisation of industry would metamorphose into 'the cartelisation of foreign policy'. From this Kautsky hoped that the worst consequences of imperialism could be mitigated.[4]

The optimism implicit in Kautsky's analysis was not, however, shared by all Marxists, and we can trace their opposition to it back to a fundamentally different conception of the nature of capitalism. Whereas Hilferding, Kautsky and others analysed capitalism as a series of national forms, Marxists like Rosa Luxemburg began from the premise that capitalism could only exist as a world economy. Capital in general is world capital and the competition of many capitals therefore transcends national boundaries as a world competition in which the state form itself plays a subordinate role. This view was implicit in Luxemburg's *Accumulation of Capital*, but it has been overshadowed by the controversy that the book generated over her discussion of capitalist crisis. It is most sharply stated in the first chapter of her *Introduction to Economics* where she devastatingly attacks 'the concept of national economy' which 'is the cornerstone on which all the works on economics written by the official representatives of this science are built.' For Luxemburg,

today, nothing is as striking, nothing of such decisive importance for the shaping of social and political life as the glaring contradiction between the economic groundwork, which daily grows stronger and more closely knit, which daily unites all peoples and all lands into one large entity — and the political superstructures, the national states which attempt to divide humanity into alien hostile portions, by artificial means, by border lines, tariff barriers and militarism.[5]

Luxemburg was not alone in developing this type of argument; it is implicit, for instance, in Trotsky's analysis at this time but it was she who gave it its most coherent first formulation, a formulation that is very similar to that of Marx in his then unknown *Grundrisse*.

It was against this background of theoretical debate that Bukharin first made his mark as a Marxist. Forced to flee from Russia in 1911, his immediate interests lay in participation in the debates on value theory and the nature of capitalist crisis. Responding to the challenge that the marginalist revolution in economics had displaced the labour theory of value, he began to lay the foundations for what he hoped would be a comprehensive critique of new trends in bourgeois economics and a vindication of Marx.[6] But the outbreak of the first world war forced his attention to more immediate events. It now became imperative to develop an analysis of what had driven capitalism to war and how Marxists should react to the effective collapse of the Second International. In doing this Bukharin's point of departure was exactly the same as that of Rosa Luxemburg, namely that capitalism can only be understood as a world system, a world economy with a world division of labour. The essentials of this argument were presented in his book *The World Economy and Imperialism* published in 1917.[7] Subsequently, he extended and developed his analysis of world capitalism over the next 13 years and an understanding of his arguments here forms the basis for an appreciation of his analysis of the nature of capitalism and socialism.

The Capitalist World Economy

For Bukharin 'modern capitalism is world capitalism' and 'social economy finds its concrete expression in world economy'.[8] In this sense the world economy was more than just the sum of its parts as was implied in the analysis of Hilferding and Kautsky and explicitly developed in the various analyses of conventional social science. On the contrary, Bukharin argued that the world economy is 'a really existing' unit which imposes its own dynamic on its parts so that 'we may define world economy as a system of production relations and, correspondingly, of exchange relations on a world scale.' The roots of this world economy lie in the expansive nature of capital itself. The competitive drive of capitals to maintain their rates of profit does not stop at national boundaries — it makes nonsense of them. Capitalism does not 'spill over' its national limits, it is by definition international. Thus the world economy does not simply exist at the level of international trade. This is only 'one of the most primitive forms of expressing production relations'. It also exists at the level of movements of labour and capital, the development of international forms like multinational companies, and so on. At the root of this lies the system of world production relations,

> the whole process of world economic life reduces itself to the production of surplus value and its distribution among various groups and sub-groups of the bourgeoisie on the basis of an ever-widening reproduction of relations between two classes — the class of the world proletariat, on the one hand, and the world bourgeoisie on the other.[9]

But if the world economy acts upon its parts then so do the parts act decisively to affect the character of the whole. While capitalism may be international, 'the process of the internationalisation of economic life is by no means identical with the process of the internationalisation of the interests of capital.' The interests of individual units of capital are determined by their competitive relations with one another. On the one hand, this gives rise to various international forms like international cartels and multinational companies. However, because capitalism is subject to recurring crises of production it also gives rise to intensified competition and problems in the reproduction of capital. As a result, individual capitals will run for cover and group around the national form for protection; that is, the state. There is thus a tendency for capitals to centralise and integrate with the state leading towards what Bukharin termed *state capitalism*. The world economy is therefore the 'special medium in which the "national economic organisms" live and grow, which conditions the nature of the economic conflict between them.'[10]

The organisational forms of the world economy are therefore the product of two contradictory forces stemming from the nature of capital. On the one hand, there is a constant tendency towards *internationalisation*, towards the breaking-down of barriers and, on the other, there is a constant trend towards *nationalisation* and the erection of barriers towards the competitive expansion of other capitals. Both tendencies are a product of the drive of capitals to accumulate and maintain their rates of profit against one another.

These tendencies do not assume an either/or form. Bukharin insisted throughout his life that the alternative to internationalisation is not autarky. This is only the most short-term solution to the problems of a particular group of capitals, it can only be the prelude to a further period of aggressive expansion. When he spoke of the nationalisation of economic life he had in mind this forced-outward development of the national form on a world scale. The contrast, then, is between the international division of labour with its international integration of production and the national drive for world power by statified capitals — this latter being only a particular historical expression of the former. What determines the shift from one to the other is the extent of the maturation of the contradictions of capitalism.[11]

As capitalism develops its problems intensify and the contrast between the international character of the system and its national form becomes more acute. Periodic crises force capital to centralise and to lean on the national political form for protection at home and abroad. The state steps in to aid the fight of its own capital for sales markets, raw materials and spheres of investment. This forces the development of new competitive forms. Commodity competition becomes distorted by monopoly and state intervention and it gives way to political and military trials of strength. Moreover, since every effort at 'national' protection is also a barrier to the expansion of other capitals and state capitals, then this competition threatens to end in war; in 1914-1918 it did so.

Writing in the midst of the first world war Bukharin put his greatest stress on the extent to which the nationalisation of economic life had triumphed. In the 1920s he was forced to qualify his analysis and to place a greater weight on the way in which the forces of internationalisation could subvert national barriers. But he regarded any suggestion that the internationalisation of capital could triumph over tendencies towards nationalisation as utopian. It is the latter that will always have the upper hand. Forms of international organisation, like international cartels, or political forms like the League of Nations, did exist but they were incomparably weaker than national forms. They faced greater organisational problems and were therefore much less stable. Disparities in production costs and rates of profit meant that any agreements around them were only temporary and with the state a potential source of monopoly profit it remained a counter-pole of attraction. Moreover, since the degree of attraction is directly related to the rate of expansion of capital, it follows that when this falls so will the strain on international bodies increase. The weaker the capital and the sharper the crisis the more it will need the support of 'its' state.[12]

In this way Bukharin argued that the world economy is 'just as blindly irrational and "subjectless" as the earlier system of *national* economy'. The crisis mechanism of the world economy is international and its ramifications are necessarily felt throughout the system. And, as the crisis develops, this anarchy results in war which 'is only one of the methods of capitalist competition when the latter extends to the sphere of world economy.'[13]

The Development and Significance of the World Economy

For Bukharin then the world economy was not an abstract concept to be imposed upon the history of capitalism. Rather, just as capital develops through the world economy so also does the world economy itself develop through the development of capital. In this dialectical fashion the world economy has grown both in breadth and depth throughout the history of capitalism. Bukharin characterised the former process as one of 'extensive' growth. At the time of the industrial revolution the capitalist world economy was virtually identical with the Atlantic economy with India on its periphery. By the time of the first world war it had drawn in virtually the whole geographical extent of the world. Bukharin closely identified this process with the rise of European colonialism. Here his historical argument does need qualification. It is true that by 1914, 84 per cent of the land area of the world was — or at one time had been — a colony of Europe. But the development of the world economy was more complex than this. Already, before the scramble for empires at the end of the nineteenth century, the extensive development of the world economy had widened the international division of labour. Certainly, colonialism extended it further still in some areas of the world but its real significance lay more in the way in which it imposed this division in a particular form, by removing power from the periphery of the world economy to sections of the bourgeoisie at the core. Moreover, once established, this division of labour had a considerable momentum of its own which allowed formal colonies to be dispensed with in the favourable climate of expansion of the three decades after the ending of the second world war.

This extensive growth of the world economy was accompanied by a massive intensification of economic relations within it which tied the fortunes of various 'national capitalisms' ever closer together. On the eve of the first world war there had developed in Europe what one historian has termed 'an immense and elaborate network of economic interdependence'.[14] Disrupted by two world wars and the 1929 world crisis these links were never broken, merely recast amidst crisis. Subsequently they have intensified still further in the period since 1945. One indicator of this is the relationship between the growth of output and trade. In Europe, for instance, since 1840 output per head has increased some sevenfold while exports per head have grown some 28-fold. Moreover, this intensification of interdependence has been heavily concentrated in the advanced countries; the Third World still remains substantially an appendage at the periphery of the world economy.[15]

But this interdependence is sunk even deeper into production relations than through trade. It is also reflected in the existence of international capital and labour markets too. The pattern set in the nineteenth century continues to operate today. Between 1821 and 1924, for example, some 55 million people crossed the Atlantic and a further 50 million moved in search of work in plantations and mines in the tropics; and this is to say nothing of the movement over land. Since 1945 this massive mobility of labour, often dictated by marginal differences in wage rates, has been re-established as a crucial feature of the development of capitalism as it has created and drawn upon a reserve army of labour on a world scale. Similarly, by 1914 some 44 billion dollars of capital had been invested abroad. This massive expansion of capital investment and accumulation on a world scale has continued at an even faster rate since 1945. The larger part of it has been in the form of direct investment by individual capitals with the result that, to take one illustration, over half of all United States trade is now between subsidiaries of the same companies.[16]

To maintain this world economy an elaborate technology is needed which Bukharin described at some length. Geographical barriers are destroyed by the expansion of capitalism and reduced to a simple time factor. The development of transport is the crucial hinge on which the world economy turns. As Marx had already put it, some 60 years before Bukharin, capitalism causes 'the annihilation of space by time'.[17]

Bukharin stressed that the significance of all this was not merely quantitative. The point is not to write a history of international economic relations, it is to get at the dynamic of capitalism. In this context the relations of the world economy play a crucial qualitative role. The world economy is 'a real totality', an 'unorganised unity' which ties its parts into complex but common rhythms of growth. These depend ultimately upon the rate of expansion in the cores. The pattern was set as early as 1847 when, for example, the crisis of that year (which was precipitated by a banking crash and panic in London) threw workers out of work not only in Britain but across industrial Europe to the Urals as well as across the Atlantic in the United States.

Capital is reorganised and restructured on a world scale through the world economy. It is this which dictates the 'national' pattern of development. This is reflected in the existence of world market prices whose development Bukharin charted. As a result 'to a very large extent "national" and local differences are levelled out in the general resultant of world prices which, in their turn, exert pressure on individual producers, individual countries, individual territories.' In so far as local differences persist then, these too can only be understood in relation to world prices through, for example, transport difficulties. The existence of world market prices for commodities is reinforced by a world price for capital, settled in the various financial markets of the world. Together these forces act to reduce value to a common scale, 'to socially necessary labour on a world scale'.[18]

The consequence of this is that no state has the capacity to control its 'national economy' because it is fractured and subordinated at so many points by the dynamic of the world economy as a whole. The idea of a 'national crisis' of capitalism is thus fallacious. The crisis exists at the level of the world economy, not the national economy. States can try to mediate and control the effects of this crisis but they cannot eliminate it. They can protect, subsidise, guarantee markets and even nationalise, but the penalties of failing to restructure production in line with the world economy remain. And not the least of these is the risk of reproducing the crisis at a higher and more politicised level as their rivals respond in kind.[19] To see the significance of this we must turn to Bukharin's analysis of imperialism.

The World Economy and Imperialism

The idea of imperialism is as central to Bukharin's analysis as it is to Lenin's. Unfortunately, however, the discussion of this has been confused by the erection of a strawman version of what they actually argued. This defines imperialism as colonialism, symbolised by the 'scramble for Africa' at the end of the nineteenth century. It is then suggested that both Bukharin and Lenin attributed this to the power of monopolistic finance capital which, in order to survive, was forced to export surplus goods and capital which could not find employment in domestic markets. Given this interpretation it is then relatively easy to show that monopolies were not far advanced in the 1880s and the 1890s; that there was no surplus of goods and capital; that trade and the export of capital did not 'follow the flag' but were concentrated in the advanced regions. The problem with all this is that it bears little or no relation to what Bukharin or Lenin argued.[20]

In the first place, neither of them understood the term imperialism to mean simply colonialism. Indeed, Bukharin explicitly rejects this, 'it is customary to reduce imperialism to colonial conquests alone. This [is an] entirely erroneous conception.' Consequently, they were not concerned to offer detailed explanations of the colonial movement. In fact, their focus of attention was the process which had driven capitalism to war in the early twentieth century, and which they expected would drive it to war again; in other words, the focus was the changes that had occurred after the 'scramble for Africa'.[21]

Bukharin analyses imperialism as an 'historical category', 'a definite historical entity'. It is the term he uses to characterise the particular form which the process of capitalist competition assumes at a specific stage of its development. This is the period when the forces of centralisation and concentration have developed to such an extent that the competitive struggle is conducted by 'state organisations of definite groups of the bourgeoisie'. It is the policy of finance capital in the sense that finance capital expresses this interpenetration of industry, banks and the state.

This competitive struggle is not new in itself. As we have seen, capital has always competed within the world economy. It is therefore wrong to imply, as did Hilferding and others, that imperialism was capital overflowing its national boundaries. This it had always done.[22] What imperialism as an historical category represented was the open emergence of an already immanent contradiction in capitalism between national and international forms. The significance of this line of analysis, and the difference from Hilferding, can be seen in the whole structure of Bukharin's book on the *World Economy and Imperialism*. There he argues from the world economy to imperialism and not the other way round. It is also clear from the title of the book but this has been obscured by its mistranslation into English as *Imperialism and the World Economy*.

What causes this contradiction to take its specific historical form of aggressive, expansionist state activity is the growing competition in the world economy. This arises because capital seeks always to buy in the cheapest markets, sell in the dearest and invest in the most profitable. This means that decisions are based upon marginal differences in the expected profits — not upon any supposed saturation of 'domestic markets'.

> It is thus obvious that not the impossibility of doing business at home, but the race for higher rates of profit is the motive power of world capitalism. . . . It is therefore easy to understand why we observe capital export almost throughout the history of the development of capitalism.[23]

This also explains the flow of investment before 1914 to areas like the United States and Russia where the necessary infrastructure for exploitation and markets already existed.

At the turn of the twentieth century this race for higher profits came to assume dramatically new forms. Capital was being accumulated in a greater volume in an increasingly monopolistic situation. This intensified competition and stimulated state action. State action was further encouraged by the dramatic impact that the restructuring of capital had upon the balance of power. Britain was increasingly challenged by both Germany and the United States at the same time as countries like Italy and Russia were struggling to gain footholds on the world market.

This increased competition found expression at all stages in the process of production. It was an intensified competition for labour power and raw materials which could lead to preclusive annexation. It was also competition for investment opportunities and, thirdly, it was competition for markets to realise surplus value. Now, however, the increasing use of 'defensive' measures like tariffs as aggressive weapons against other capitals injected a new political element into the process. In the years before 1914 the process of 'internationalisation' consequently proceeded apace with and through the process of 'nationalisation'.

> When competition has finally reached its highest stage, when it has become competition between state capitalist trusts, then the use of state power and the possibilities connected with it begin to play a very large part . . . [in this way] the internationalisation of economic life here, too, makes it necessary to settle controversial questions by fire and sword.[24]

This conflict, however, is not simply economic. In order to sustain the role of the capitalist state in an era of imperialism it is also necessary to develop aggressive ideological forms based upon the mystique of the 'nation'. In this way a wholly irrational political element is injected into the system. But it is an irrationality that can have such a devastating effect precisely because it is on the basis of the tendency towards state capitalism that politics intertwine with economics. Bukharin then did not reduce imperialism to a simple matter of economics. What he did was to show that when politics did intervene, it did so because of the economic changes that had gone beforehand. This led him to reject the argument, later made famous by Schumpeter, that imperialism was a product of the survival of 'feudal' elements. On the contrary, he argued that it was not a matter of survival but of capitalism at its most advanced level which gives expression to the barbaric idea of 'a self-sufficient national state, and an economic unit limitlessly expanding its great power until it becomes a world kingdom — a world-wide empire — such is the ideal built by finance capital.'[25]

The Role of War

The consequence of this is the constant threat of world war. War plays an important role in Bukharin's analysis, in the sense that he sees it as the highest form of capitalist competition: 'A mighty state military power is the last trump in the struggle of the powers.' It is this that makes the choice of 'barbarism or socialism' such a terrifying one. Capitalism creates 'narrow "national" groups armed to the teeth and ready to hurl themselves at one another at any moment'; it leads to 'millions of butchered workers, to billions devoured by the war, to the monstrous pressure of brazen militarism, to the vandalism of productive forces, to the high cost of living and starvation!'[26]

But war is not simply an armed conflict. Bukharin argued that it 'serves to reproduce definite relations of production', it occurs 'in the space of a given mode of production'. Capitalist war intensifies the key contradictions of capitalism and reproduces them on a higher and more barbaric level. In this way 'war is a special form of capitalist competition.'[27]

The importance of this argument is not hard to follow in the light of the recent history of capitalism, though Marxists have generally paid little attention to the theoretical significance of the war economy (as opposed to arms spending) for their analysis of capitalism. Yet not only have wars become more devastating but they are also more frequent. At one level, with the emergence of the Cold War, a war economy has been built into the heart of the 'peacetime economies' of the advanced world. Amongst the poorer countries of the 'post-war' world the wars have been 'hot'. At the beginning of the 1980s something of the order of one-sixth of the world's population was at war, and this proportion probably held for most of the previous decade and, if anything, threatens to increase.

The difficulty is that the war economy seems to suppress what many have judged to be the defining characteristics of capitalism. States intervene, control, rationalise, centralise and nationalise; they destroy or eliminate markets in favour of administrative allocation and the rationing of raw materials, labour and capital and final goods in aid of the war effort. This can be seen most obviously in the history of the first and second world wars and in the economies of the inter-war fascist regimes, but it is equally present in the war-machines of the modern world. In terms of its economic power, the world's second largest 'planned' economy, after the Soviet Union, is to be found not behind the Iron Curtain but behind the doors of the Pentagon.[28]

Here it would be difficult to speak of capitalism as a form of generalised commodity production as some Marxists have done. Equally it would be difficult to conceive of it in terms of wage labour. The simple wage form has been commonly distorted in war economies, and in Nazi Germany a significant part of war production regressed to the use of slave labour. Certainly, many contemporaries interpreted such changes as these in the first and second world wars as signs of 'war socialism'. Others, less sanguine, saw them as a part of a new feudalism.

But such conceptions rest upon the attempt to give capitalism a simple, finished and abstract definition. What Bukharin did was to show that these changes do not alter the capitalist nature of the system. Having produced war, capitalism does not then negate itself. The central drive to expand value becomes intensified and in the process accentuates particular elements of capitalism while suppressing others. In this way he saw war as capitalist competition by other means. Just as capitalist competition generally acts to reproduce capitalist relations of production so does capitalist competition at this higher level act to reproduce what he termed 'definite relations of production'. Here is to be found not the germ of socialism but the barbarism of capitalism.

The Importance of Bukharin's Analysis

As we have seen, Bukharin was not alone in developing the argument that capitalism can only be understood as a world economy, but with the degeneration of the Russian Revolution any discussion of the significance of his analysis became impossible and it is only in more recent years that its importance has become clear. Indeed, it can be argued that much recent Marxist debate has suffered because of the continuing neglect of Bukharin and an unwillingness to explore his solutions.

It would not be true to say that there has been no discussion of capitalism as a world economy. Rather the problem continues to lie in the way that this is conceived. For orthodox economics the idea of the world economy remains a vague entity with little or no methodological significance. The national economy is still the unit of analysis and the world economy is a simple aggregate of its parts — precisely the type of perspective that Bukharin condemned. More recently there has been a welcome attempt on the Left to assert the primacy of the world economy in the analysis of capitalism. This has been particularly associated with the work of André Gunder Frank and Immanuel Wallerstein who have produced a number of historical and contemporary analyses of the development of capitalism.[29] In so far as both these writers have gone beyond merely radicalising the existing analyses produced by orthodox historians their work raises intriguing questions for Marxists. But there nevertheless remains an important defect in their analysis which makes it suspect and inferior in its theoretical conception to Bukharin's analysis.

The essence of this problem lies in the way in which the world economy is analysed through the use of various arbitrary and descriptive categories of a more or less static character like those of 'the core, semi-periphery and periphery'. The primacy of the general category, the world economy and these sub-categories over the national form is then asserted more often than analysed. Moreover, in so far as their idea of a world economy has any analytical content it seems to rest upon the primacy of exchange relations.

From the point of view of a Marxist analysis these are grave defects.[30] In contrast, Bukharin emphasises that the world economy is founded on relations of production to which relations of exchange are subordinate. He then goes on to derive the forms of the world economy from the dynamic of capital itself. In this way, for example, the debate over whether internal or external determinants account for the nature of the national form is rendered illusory. Both have to be seen as different moments of the same processes which serve to reinforce one another. Obviously Bukharin's analysis is not complete; it exists only in outline. But it is difficult to see how a satisfactory analysis can be made which ignores his work in this area.

A related example of the failure satisfactorily to explore the nature of capitalism as a world economy can be found in the extensive debate on the capitalist state. Only now is this discussion beginning to confront the fact that capitalism exists as a multiplicity of states within the world economy. The major part of the discussion has displaced the world economy to a secondary factor and focused on the state itself as the basic unit of analysis. The consequence of this, as von Braumuhl and Barker have pointed out, is that an analysis which claims to lay bare the foundation of the state begins by assuming what it needs to explain – the differentiation of capital into 'national forms'.[31] If one follows Bukharin's lead, one which von Braumuhl implicitly suggests has its foundations in Marx, a different set of questions are posed. In the first place, to quote von Braumuhl,

> the task before us is to explain [the differentiation of the world market] as national capitals and its organisation as nation states. . . . It is not just a question of the state in general, but of the derivation of the specific political organisation of the world market in many states, or, in other words, of explaining the particularisation of capital in national capitals each with their own particular organs and their own features.[32]

Secondly, in explaining this apparent conflict between 'nationalisation' and 'internationalisation', both have to be seen as being determined not simply by historical circumstance but by the process of accumulation. For example, it is not possible simply to counterpose forms like the multinational company to the nation-state or to present supra-national organisations like the EEC as challengers to national integrity which cast doubt on the viability of the national form. The interests of the multinational company and the supra-national organisation are certainly not identical with those of the nation-state but neither are they completely separate. The development of all these forms is the product of the general process of the concentration of capital as capitalism as a system matures. In this way they each underpin and reinforce the other. This is why, when competition in the world economy intensifies, the apparently footloose multinational companies quickly find that they do have national flags, because these are now needed to give them the *national* power to maintain their *international* position.[33]

Thirdly, the fact that we can now see a multiplicity of national capitals means that it can no longer be argued that the state represents the interests of 'capital in general'. At best it can be said that the state represents no more than the interests of a particular group of capitals against another group of capitals. But even this must be qualified to recognise the way in which the state, as capital, represents its own interest as well.[34]

These are relatively abstract issues. But Bukharin's analysis also led him to two more directly political conclusions. At the time that he first put forward his analysis he directed much of his fire against the idea that the centralisation of capital could proceed to such an extent that a single, all-embracing trust could be formed and dominate the world. This argument is rarely found today and even fewer would deduce from it the possibility of some kind of capitalist world government as did some of Bukharin's contemporaries. But echoes of this argument can be found in the writing on the multinational company. Here it has been seriously argued that these have detached themselves from the state and broken its 'integrity'. For Bukharin this type of argument, in any form, simply represented wishful thinking. The essence of capitalism as a world economy is that it is torn *both* by forces making for the internationalisation *and* the nationalisation of economic life. Because of this there can be no basis within capitalism for a genuinely international solution to its problems. This can only come about in a socialist world.

But this argument had, and has, a more pointed corollary in the other direction too. If there can be no international solution to the problems of capitalism within capitalism then neither can there be a national solution. For the reasons we have outlined, attempts to find such national solutions behind tariff walls only intensify conflict and competition on a world scale. At a time when some of Bukharin's arguments have been taken up by those on the European Left who advocate various national remedies, it is important to stress both how much their policies are in contradiction with his own analysis and how alien he would have found their philosophies and programmes. Far from seeing socialism as the logical culmination of state capitalism on a national scale, Bukharin saw it as its negation. To see why, it is necessary to turn and explore his analysis of the capitalist state in some detail.

Notes

1. G. Hardach, D. Karras and B. Fine, *A Short History of Socialist Economic Thought*, London: Edward Arnold, 1978, chapters 3 and 4.

2. K. Marx, *Capital*, vol. 1, Harmondsworth, Middlesex: Penguin Books, 1976, p. 727.

3. R. Rosdolsky, *The Making of Marx's 'Capital'*, London: Pluto Press, 1977.

4. K. Kautsky, 'Ultra-Imperialism', *New Left Review*, no. 59 January/February 1970.

5. R. Luxemburg, *What is Economics?*, Colombo Ceylon: Young Socialist, 1968, p. 43.

6. N.I. Bukharin, *The Economic Theory of the Leisure Class*, New York: Monthly Review Press, 1972; D. Maretskii, 'Nikolai Ivanovich Bukharin', *Bol'shaya sovetskaya entsiklopediya*, 1st edn, vol. viii, Moscow, 1926.

7. N.I. Bukharin, *Imperialism and the World Economy*, London: Merlin, 1972. For some reason the title was reversed in the English translation. The difference is of some significance for the argument. Hereafter it will be referred to as *World Economy*.

8. N.I. Bukharin, *The Economics of the Transformation Period*, New York: Bergman, 1971 (hereafter *Economics*), pp. 12-13. References are given to this edition, in spite of the fact that it is a poor translation (the title is more normally given as *Transition Period*), because it contains Lenin's comments on the book.

9. *World Economy*, pp. 25-7.

10. Ibid., p. 61; *Economics*, chapters 1-3.

11. This theme was being developed by Bukharin as late as 1935-36; see his 'Imperialism and Communism', *Foreign Affairs*, vol. XIV, no. 4, July 1936.

12. *World Economy*, chapter 12.

13. *Economics*, p. 19; *World Economy*, p. 54.

14. W. Ashworth, 'Industrialisation and the Economic Integration of Nineteenth-century Europe', *European Studies Review*, vol. iv, no. 4, 1974.

15. Estimates in constant prices for 1840-1970 based on data collected by Paul Bairoch.

16. N. Harris, *Of Bread and Guns. The World Economy in Crisis*, Harmondsworth, Middlesex: Penguin Books, 1983; N. Harris, 'The Road from 1910', *Economy and Society*, vol. 11, no. 3, August 1982.

17. K. Marx, *Grundrisse*, Harmondsworth, Middlesex: Penguin Books, 1973, p. 539; *World Economy*, pp. 34-6.

18. Ibid., pp. 23-5.

19. N.I. Bukharin, 'Nekotorye problemy sovremennogo kapitalizma u teoretikov burzhuazii', in *'Organizovannyi kapitalizm'*, Moscow: Communist Academy, 1930, p. 176.

20. For this view, see D.K. Fieldhouse, *The Theory of Capitalist Imperialism*, London: Longman, 1967. For a general corrective, see E. Stokes, 'Late Nineteenth-century Colonial Expansion and the Attack on the Theory of Economic Imperialism', *Historical Journal*, vol. xii, no. 2, 1969.

21. *World Economy*, p. 121.

22. See, for example, R. Hilferding, *Finance Capital*, London: Routledge & Kegan Paul, 1981, chapters 21-2.

23. *World Economy*, pp. 84, 96; N.I. Bukharin, 'Imperialism and the Accumulation of Capital', in R. Luxemburg and N.I. Bukharin, *Imperialism and the Accumulation of Capital*, London: Allen Lane, 1972, pp. 238-57.

24. *World Economy*, pp. 123-4, 103.

25. Ibid., p. 109.

26. Ibid., pp. 107, 167.
27. Ibid., p. 121; *Economics*, p. 30; 'Imperialism and Communism', *op. cit.*, p. 576.
28. H. Sherman, *Radical Political Economy*, New York: Basic Books, 1972, pp. 143-4.
29. See, for example, A.G. Frank, *Dependent Accumulation and Underdevelopment*, London: Macmillan, 1978; I. Wallerstein, *The Modern World System*, New York: Academic Press, 1974.
30. J. Banaji, 'Modes of Production in a Materialist Conception of History', *Capital and Class*, no. 3, Autumn 1977.
31. C. von Braumuhl, 'On the Bourgeois Nation State within the World Market', in J. Holloway and S. Picciotto (eds), *State and Capital*, London: Edward Arnold, 1978; C. Barker, 'A Note of the Theory of Capitalist States', *Capital and Class*, no. 4, Spring 1978.
32. von Braumuhl, *op. cit.*, pp. 164, 166.
33. See the debate in Radice, *op. cit.*; and S. Sagall, 'The Crisis and the Multinationalisation of Capital', *International Socialism* (second series), no. 6, Autumn 1979.
34. Barker, *op. cit.*; and C. Barker, 'The State as Capital', *International Socialism* (second series), no. 1, July 1978.

3 CAPITAL AND THE STATE

In recent years there has been a welcome rebirth in the Marxist theory of the state. One result of this has been a major advance in the understanding of the capitalist state. The importance of Bukharin's contribution to this issue has been summed up by two historians of Marxist political economy. Bukharin's analysis, they write,

> raises a problem that is central within theoretical discussion today, namely the role of the state in the process of reproduction of capital . . . the state is not an institution standing above the capital relation, it is not independent of the conflict between capital and labour; the state for Bukharin is dependent on the development of capital and has to be explained from it.[1]

Yet in spite of this, much of the debate has taken place in ignorance of Bukharin's contribution. Not the least of the reasons for this has been the continuing impact of the propaganda that was put out to discredit Bukharin's whole analysis after his defeat by Stalin in 1929. This propaganda attempted to show both that Bukharin had always been in dispute with Lenin on the question of the state, and that he had come to adopt the idea of 'organised capitalism' developed in the 1920s by Rudolph Hilferding. Both charges are without foundation although it is still common to find them made today.

The situation of Bukharin's relationship to Lenin was thoroughly confused in the 1930s as the need to attack Bukharin led to the creation of a particular version of Lenin's argument in which every criticism of Bukharin, every nuance of expression, was blown up into a major theoretical issue. Yet, if we penetrate behind this smokescreen, it soon becomes apparent that Lenin's analysis of the capitalist state converged closely with that of Bukharin. Although Lenin often developed his analysis by a different route and showed a greater and more acute understanding of the politics of the state, by 1917 they had come to share an essentially common view of its role in capitalism. Lenin's main difference with Bukharin related not so much to this issue as that of the post-revolutionary situation in Russia. What he did do on a number of occasions was to correct Bukharin when he thought that he had implied that the tendencies towards the growth of the capitalist state had gone further than they had. But these 'inexact' formulations of Bukharin did not stop his recommending Bukharin's 'splendid work', *The Economics of the Transition Period*, where the analysis of the state and capital is developed in full, as 'indispensable to our reading public'. The defects of what Lenin saw as an occasional lapse into scholasticism or, more sharply, Bukharin's excessively 'sociological' (or undialectical) focus were no more than 'a spoonful of tar in a barrel of honey'. Lenin was equally warm in the introduction he wrote to Bukharin's *World Economy and Imperialism*.[2] Moreover, after 1917 Bukharin's analysis came to be recognised as an essential component of Bolshevik thinking until the tradition in which he was so involved was overturned by Stalin.

The other charge — that Bukharin shared Hilferding's analysis of 'organised capitalism' — has no more substance, but this can best be dealt with by situating Bukharin's analysis of the state against the background of discussion in the Second International. Far from sharing or appropriating Hilferding's analysis, Bukharin was, in fact, one of his major critics.

A General Theory of the State

Orthodox Marxists at the Second International did not doubt that the state was a class institution. However, the analysis behind this and the conclusions they drew from it were significantly different from Marx's own position. What determined the class nature of the state for them was the control that the ruling class exercised over it. The state was not seen as a direct consequence of capital as a social relation but indirectly, through the existence of social classes. The state appeared as an object in their analysis, it was an 'instrument' that was wielded by the ruling class. This 'instrumentalist' conception was shared by the majority of the Second International. The debates of the time tended to turn on the issue of the degree of control exercised by the ruling class. For a revisionist like Eduard Bernstein, the working class could roll back the ruling class and bend the state to its will. For a defender of orthodoxy like Karl Kautsky, this was not possible short of a revolution which would allow the working class control of the state until its final abolition with the emergence of true communism. Both sides pictured the state as having autonomy from capitalism as a mode of production (since it could transcend it) but totally subordinate to classes whose instrument it was.

This view of the state had two immediate political consequences for the analysis of the transition to socialism. The first was that the existing state form could continue after the revolution and, indeed, perhaps needed to be developed to a higher degree. The second was that the general vision of socialism became increasingly identified with a rationalised, centralised and state-controlled society. The question of the 'withering away of the state' was passed to a society of the future so distant as to be irrelevant. This was a constant strain of thought amongst western social-democrats. In Russia it was destroyed in the writings of Marxists like Bukharin and Lenin, only to be reborn in the 1920s and embodied in the basic ideology of an emerging Stalinism. Just as it had been by Lassalle in Marx's time, socialism was reduced to nationalisation and state control.

The way in which the particular logic of this conception of the state was drawn out can be seen in the development of Hilferding's analysis. For Hilferding the concentration of capital led to an 'organised capitalism' in which the state played the leading role by suppressing the most basic features of capitalism like the market and the category of profit. By the 1920s Hilferding was drawn to the conclusion that 'organised capitalism means the replacement of the capitalist principle of free competition by the socialist principle of planned production.'[3] Capitalism was developing into socialism as part of the logic of its own development. With others of his fellow Austro-Marxists like Otto Bauer, Hilferding saw these developments as reflecting a transcendent rationality which led to the victory of socialism. This idea was concisely expressed by Bauer when he argued that 'rationalisation' under capitalism led to a 'style of thought [which] avoids everything that cannot be calculated; it shuns every risk, every uncertain adventure.' Here lay the possibility of peaceful advance, as the socialists gained support as organisation increased so would the pressure of 'rationalisation' prevent any violent reaction against the advance. 'Modern democracy is rooted in this style of thought,' wrote Bauer and it could not be overturned.[4] The shock that the success of the Nazi regime inflicted on this optimistic view of progress hardly needs to be pointed to.

Elements of an instrumentalist view of the state are not entirely absent from some of Bukharin's writings. As a leading publicist of the Bolshevik cause, he was as prone as any Marxist to dwell on the machinations of the capitalist class and to stress the more obvious links of some of their members to the capitalist state. But this was not the core of his analysis. Alongside the inevitable crudities and simplifications of daily propaganda there exists a much more sophisticated analysis of the state which led him to break with the kind of thinking represented by the theoreticians of the Second International at two levels. First, he quickly came to the conclusion that the state must be seen as more than just a coercive force, and that it cannot simply be identified with the superstructure of society. Secondly, he argued that, in explaining the form of the state, it is above all necessary to relate it to the basic dynamic of capital. The former emphasis took him very near to Gramsci as has recently been recognised.[5] The latter emphasis, however, divided him from Gramsci both by suggesting a different starting point for his analysis and, ultimately, a different vision of the future of the state and capital.

Bukharin's contribution developed through two stages. The first was an act of recovery of Marx's analysis which was subsequently overshadowed by Lenin's own contribution in *State and Revolution*. Bukharin not only preceded Lenin here but it was his own work which was one of the key factors stimulating Lenin's rethinking on the state.[6] Since this argument has become familiar through Lenin it will suffice here merely to note the outlines of what Bukharin had to say.

Contrary to those who argued that the state existed as an expression of the general good, Bukharin argued that

> for Marx, the *essence* of the state is . . . that it is an organisation of oppression, domination, exploitation, a weapon and organisation of the *dominating class*. In exactly the same way as *capital*, for Marx, is not a general means of production but a means of production monopolised by the *dominating class*, so also is the state *not* a general organisation but an organisation in the hands of the dominating class. But as socialism is the abolition of classes then this means also the abolition of the state.[7]

This early passage is doubly interesting because it shows the way in which Bukharin could break with fundamental aspects of the thinking of the Second International while remaining tied to other aspects. The conclusion and the interpretation of Marx is radical, and to support it Bukharin drew attention to Marx's neglected writings on the need to smash the state. The formulation of the argument, however, remains trapped at this time within an instrumentalist view of the world. Fortunately, Bukharin did not rest content with this.

Marx's analysis, he argued, went further. Marx provided 'an historical method of investigation of social phenomena' which enabled the specific forms they took to be unravelled. This is necessary because not only does the form of the state differ between capitalist and pre-capitalist modes but it also changes under capitalism.[8] This question had become increasingly important in the decades before the first world war. These had seen a dramatic increase in the level of state activity. Bukharin argued that this had to be seen in relation to the development of capital as a social relation. This again took him further away from the thinking of the Second International where the question of the form of the state was increasingly separated from its class content. For Bukharin, what was necessary was to explain both the class content of the state and its class form.

It was precisely this link of content and form that Bukharin found lacking in the analysis of Hilferding and Bauer. Hilferding, he argued, had merely alighted on certain features of modern capitalism, most notably the tendency to attempt to organise the national economy, but he had failed to see that 'this tendency to organisation is developing into antagonistic, contradictory forms.' The anarchy of production was not being overcome under capitalism but '*intensified*, although actually changed in its *form* . . . into a concentrated struggle of imperialist monsters with the world as its battlefield.' It could not result in a society, as Hilferding hoped, 'without crisis and unemployment, with a steady and wisely regulated wage'.[9]

This link between the class content of the state and its class form led directly to Bukharin's political conclusion that the state was not an autonomous actor from capitalism. The capitalist state could not be cut adrift from its class base, it would not grow into socialism. Revolution would have to smash both the class content of the state and its class form, replacing it with a new and qualitatively different type of temporary state, the dictatorship of the proletariat which we shall examine in the next chapter.

Bukharin's attempt to relate the state to the development of capitalism raises the question of his theory of capitalist crisis since it is crisis which intensifies the competition which leads to the structural and institutional changes he discussed. To pursue this fully would take us into areas of Marxist political economy which are too complex to discuss here. It will be sufficient to note that in his discussion of economic crisis Bukharin was concerned to explain the cyclical pattern of capitalist development. This took him to the debates between Rosa Luxemburg and her German critics and between the under-consumptionists and the disproportionality theorists.[10] Here he argued that they all attempted to present monocausal explanations of crisis which were at fault both economically and politically. For Bukharin, crisis under capitalism was the product not of any single dominating contradiction, but a general 'unity of contradictions', both economic and political. In this debate Bukharin put forward one of the more sophisticated positions but the details of it would take us far afield and they must be traced elsewhere by interested readers.[11]

What is important for us about this debate is the way that both Bukharin and the majority of his contemporaries allowed a key problem to go by default. This is the question of Marx's analysis of the falling rate of profit, an area that had been little recognised by the economists of the Second International. Bukharin (whose formulation of Marx's argument has a distinctively modern ring) certainly knew of it but he failed to provide any discussion of it in relation to capitalist crisis. When he did introduce the possibility of a long-term decline in the rate of profit it was in a completely untheorised way.[12] In this sense there is an important element of incompleteness in his discussion by modern standards. The state is seen as subordinate to the development of capital as a relation of production. This in turn is founded upon competition, but here he only explains the periodic intensification of competition, not any long-term trends. The result is that the analysis of competition seems to hang in the air.

The problem of crisis theory, however, is subordinate to the controversy created by Bukharin's general discussion of the state, and it is this that we must explore in detail. The controversy has arisen partly because the conclusions he drew still seem unpalatable to many on the Left and partly because his critics have not always been clear about the method by which he reached them. It is important to say something about this latter issue before looking at the actual analysis.

Bukharin was concerned to try to understand the basic dynamic of capitalism. This led him to consider 'all phenomena in their pure form' as a 'pure model'.[13] Driving beyond the specifics of each case, he tried to draw out the essence of the tendencies he analysed. There is no doubt that this led him, on occasion, to overestimate the degree of development of the tendencies he had identified. But this is a separate issue. The key point is that he did not intend his 'algebraic formulae' to be understood as descriptions of reality. (In arguing, for instance, that capitalism tends towards state capitalism he did not argue that any particular society could be described as a state capitalism.) Here, he insisted, he was following Marx's method in *Capital*:

we do not at all neglect 'special features' ... there are great differences concerning *how and at what speed* the forces of the statification of production proceed. But we are investigating above all, not these peculiarities but the basic tendencies of development. This was also Marx's method which on the basis of the investigation of the basic laws of development of English capitalism predicted its development on the continent.[14]

It is therefore no great criticism of Bukharin to qualify his argument about the extent to which any individual tendency has developed. He accepted this type of comment on many occasions. If criticism is to have real force it must be shown either that he was wrong in his analysis of the pure model, or that the pure model was irrelevant because he had fundamentally misunderstood the tendencies. Our argument will be that while it is possible to question aspects of the model, he neverthe-less did have a correct grasp of the fundamental tendencies of capitalist development.

Capital and the State

In Chapter 2 we saw that Bukharin argued that the world economy is torn between the forces of the internationalisation and nationalisation of capital. In his analysis of the state he concentrated on the latter. This was to show the specific way in which capital became particularised in nation-states and the relation this bore to the development of the world economy. Of necessity, therefore, he began by recognising that capitalism exists in the form of many states.

Bukharin argued that the state is necessary to secure the conditions for the reproduction of capital as a social relation. This means that the state must perform a series of essential economic and political functions which go considerably beyond being a force of coercion.

> The fact is that the very foundation of modern states as definite political entities was caused by economic needs and requirements. The state grew on the economic foundation; it was only an expression of economic connections; state ties appeared only as an expression of economic ties.[15]

The formulation may be unnecessarily determinist but the thrust of the argument enabled him to begin to attempt to relate the changing form of the state to the dynamic of the capitalist system as a whole.

Bukharin argued that the conditions for the reproduction of capital were constantly changing. They had to be constantly regenerated as capital was reproduced. This gave them an historical dimension as capital developed through time. The substance of this argument was set out in an article he wrote in 1916 entitled 'Towards a Theory of the Imperialist State'. Here he examined the shift from the mercantilist state of the seventeenth and eighteenth centuries, which in Marx's phrase had acted as the 'midwife' of capitalism, to the *laissez-faire* forms which characterised the nineteenth century, and the imperialist state of the early twentieth century.[16]

The decisive factor in this transition was the way in which the concentration and centralisation of capital, under the pressure of intensified competition, led to the state being forced to assume an ever greater role in the reproduction of the conditions of existence of particular groups of capitals. This tendency found its expression in state support and regulation and state ownership. In this process the state itself became a direct capitalist:

> either the state organisation is one of *direct* exploitation – in which case the state appears as a union of capitalists, owning its own enterprises (e.g. railways, the monopolistic production of one or another product, etc.) – or, alternatively, the state organisation takes part in the process of exploitation *indirectly*, as an auxiliary mechanism for the support and maximal extension of conditions suitable for the exploitative process.... In concrete reality, both these patterns coexist, although the proportionate relation between them is subject to change and depends on the level of historical development that has been attained.

Taken to its extreme, this process could lead to the formation of national 'state capitals' where the state takes over the role of the capitalist completely, 'the logical limit of which is *state capitalism*, or the inclusion of absolutely everything within the sphere of state regulation.'[17]

It should be stressed again that Bukharin saw this as a tendency. Nevertheless, it was a tendency which the first world war 'like a gigantic crisis, has intensified'. The exact pattern, of course, varied. It went furthest in Germany, the country to which Bukharin devoted most attention.[18] But for capitalism as a whole he had no doubt that 'in so far as capitalism will retain its foothold, the future belongs to forms close to state capitalism.'[19]

In the 1920s he attempted a more precise evaluation to take account of the tendencies in peacetime. His basic position was well summed up in 1927:

> when examining the internal structure of the imperialist states and their economies we must distinguish between elements of state capitalism in western Europe which bear a specifically war character ... and the present tendencies ... in the direction of state capitalism. We see the development of state capitalist tendencies in two main directions. On the one hand (and this is the chief tendency) there is a process of the growing-together between economic organs of capital and the organs of state power 'from below' (which I have named the 'trustification of state capital'). ... On the other hand, a certain advance is also to be observed in features bearing the formal stamp of state capitalism: state undertakings, state organisation of trade unions, price regulation, etc. This process takes place 'from above'. ... It would be wrong ... to proclaim the 'era' of state capitalism. But it would be equally wrong to fail to recognise the tendencies.[20]

This intertwining of state and capital resulted in changes in the forms of competition. As the state intervened so it attempted to organise the internal economy and suppress its anarchy in order better to focus its forces on the external competition. In this way *'centralisation of capital* consumes competition, but on the other hand reproduces it on an extended base' in the world economy. In this situation it is the relationship with the world economy which acts to enforce the laws of capitalism:

> the 'economic goods' *within* the combined enterprises are put into circulation not as commodities but as products and they represent commodities only in so far as they are hurled out of the combined total complex. In the same way, the product whose distribution is organised within the nation, is only a commodity in so far as its being connected with the existence of the world market.[21]

At the same time the methods of external competition also change. Bukharin did not subsume capitalism under commodity production. He argued that the commodity is subordinate to capital and that capitalism is characterised by 'capitalist commodity production' where it is capital which is the dominant element. As the state assumes control and capitalism becomes monopolised so is simple commodity competition pushed aside in favour of the forms of competition we discussed in Chapter 2.

A third element to change was the state itself: 'With the growth of the importance of state power, its inner structure also changes.' There is a shift towards centralised power which produces 'crises of parliamentarism'. This shift in political power, from representative institutions to centralised government, raises the question of the precise role of the bourgeoisie. Bukharin argued that because the state is a social relation deriving from and maintaining capital there need be no real contradiction here. Elements of the bourgeoisie would oppose any such shifts if it meant that they were denied power. But the shift itself involved only a modification within the ranks of the bourgeoisie, not its expropriation as various revisionists like Bernstein had imagined. The social relations based on capital remain:

> the capitalist mode of production is based on a monopoly of the means of production in the hands of the class of capitalists. . . . There is no difference in principle whatsoever whether the state power is a direct expression of this monopoly or whether this monopoly is 'privately' organised. In either case there remains commodity economy (in the first place the world market) and, what is more important, the class relations between the proletariat and the bourgeoisie.

This step in Bukharin's argument is a central one because it shows that he did not make the mistake of confusing relations of production with private property as a particular legal form. On the contrary, capitalist relations of production can be 'politically perpetuated in the state organisation of capital'. It was in this sense that state capitalism was possible, but the argument also has, as we shall see later, important implications too for his analysis of the state and the transition to socialism.[22]

We have already drawn attention to the danger of reductionism in Bukharin's argument. Nevertheless, he was not unaware of this. Had he been concerned to analyse specific state forms a far more nuanced interpretation would have been necessary. But his concern here is the general tendencies. The whole thrust of his argument is that there is a necessary and historically limited relationship between the class content of the state and the class forms which it could assume. He did not deny the role of politics or of class, but attempted to show the conditions from which they derived and against which they were forced to operate.

In his book on *Historical Materialism*, for example, he shows that he is well aware of the breadth of the social and political forces which stabilise and legitimise capital. 'The social and political structure of society is not limited to the state authority. The ruling class, as well as the oppressed classes, present the most varied organisations and forms of common action.' This superstructure is 'a combination of things, persons, and ideas'. It is determined by economics in the sense that economics *conditions* classes which in turn are reflected and expressed in politics.[23] This applies no less to the state itself:

> like every 'superstructure' [the state] is not simply a glass-shade covering the economic life but an active power, an operating organisation, which secures on all sides the base of production on which it arose.[24]

But if the state cannot be reduced to the base and the dynamic of capital, neither can it be detached from it. It is this that divides Bukharin's analysis from attempts like that of Poulantzas which seek to understand the state at the political level. It also separates him from Gramsci, although Bukharin did have a concept of hegemony. Because Bukharin's analysis turns initially on the relation of capital and the state, he can go beyond seeing the state as 'the site of class compromises, the place where a power bloc is articulated and organised' to see it as a potential subject in the development of capitalism.[25] As this independent subject it can subordinate society to itself in state capitalism. The state personifies capital in the way that the private capitalist had done in the past. The fact that Bukharin's analysis opens up the possibility of the state as the object of capital but the subject of society constitutes its most important and its most controversial feature. The substantive question must therefore be the validity of this idea of state capitalism and it is to this we now turn.

The Possibility of State Capitalism

The possibility of state capitalism has been questioned and rejected at a number of levels. One of the most common criticisms was raised by Rudolf Hilferding. Faced with the argument in the 1930s that the Soviet Union was a form of state capitalism, he denied that the concept had any theoretical status in any context. It could 'scarcely pass the test of serious economic analysis'. His argument was that capitalism is based on the market, profit and private appropriation. Since state capitalism implied a partial, if not a complete, negation of these (in the sense Hilferding understood them), then it appeared to him as an absurdity. He was not blind to the ways in which these features had been qualified over the past century and here he had a consistency which some of those who followed him have lacked. In defining capitalism in terms of the market, Hilferding was concerned both to deny state capitalism and to argue that capitalism itself was already being socialised away. This, indeed, would seem to be the general dilemma of anyone who erects a definition of capitalism based upon its features at a particular stage in its development.[26]

An equally common but misdirected criticism is that capitalism can only exist on the basis of many capitals. This argument, however, in spite of being directed at Bukharin, misunderstands his position. He too made a point of denying that a single capital could ever exist in isolation. His whole argument was that this could not occur because of the existence of the world economy. State capitalism is possible because state capitals exist in a world of many capitals.

By far the most serious potential criticism, however, lies in another direction. It has been argued by a number of contributors to the Marxist debate on the state that, although the state is necessary for the reproduction of capital, it cannot itself be capital. It cannot assume the role of a direct exploiter in Bukharin's sense; a total state capital cannot exist. This criticism has been made both from a political and an economic perspective.

In terms of politics the most elegant argument has been put by Jürgen Habermas. For Habermas, advanced capitalism can only survive because of state intervention to secure further accumulation and avoid economic crisis breaking out. Without such intervention the relations of production would become so politicised that massive class conflict would ensue. However, in practising this crisis-avoidance, Habermas then argues that there are 'strict limitations' to the role of the state. These limitations are imposed by the capitalists themselves, 'the private autonomous disposition of the means of production demands a limitation to state intervention and prohibits planned coordination of the contradictory interests of individual capitalists.'[27]

This is obviously an important argument and it gains in the light of Bukharin's underestimation of the opposition of the bourgeoisie to state takeover in specific instances. In a situation of what Bukharin might have called 'social equilibrium' there will, at any given moment, be limits to the type of changes that can occur. But the limitations of

Habermas's argument are no less clear when it is made as a general argument about the relationship of capital and the state. The historical basis of the argument lies in the experience of the 1950s and the 1960s when advanced capitalism was run according to a bowdlerised version of Keynesianism. Here 'the contradictory interests of individual capitalists' certainly did prevent any genuine national planning and it gave rise to what became known as 'the political trade-cycle' as governments tried to buy themselves a further lease of life by appropriate concessions at election time. Where Habermas falls down is in his reading of the long-run tendencies of capitalism from experiences which, it can be argued, were specific to the boom of the post-war decades. What he rules out of his analysis (partly because he overrates the ability of the state to ward off crises) are crises of such depth that they so disrupt social equilibrium as to threaten 'national survival'. In such a crisis the contradictory pressures on the state and capital which normally maintain a degree of separation between them will be thrown out of balance.

There is no need to search far for evidence of this. The very fact that even amongst advanced western capitalist nations there exists a wide variation in levels of state activity around the general rising trend is itself indicative that the strict limitations on state action have been more elastic in some situations than in others. If we then go on to examine previous situations of crisis the picture becomes even clearer. One important example which is ignored by most theorists of the state (though not Bukharin, as we have seen) is that of the war economy as it developed between 1914 and 1918 and again in the second world war. Another would be that of the 1930s, when a crisis in the reproduction of capital in conditions of acute international tension and major domestic political realignments forced the bourgeoisie, or large sections of it, into the arms of the state. Then in Germany, for example, the Nazi regime gained such power as to be able fundamentally to challenge the specific interests of private capital which today Habermas sees as limiting the role of the state. Since this has happened more than once, it is difficult to see why it should be ruled out for the future, particularly as capitalism has begun to regain some of its old instability. The formation of more or less consolidated state capitalisms in the advanced West would demand a tremendous crisis, but it cannot be ruled out as an absolute impossibility; nor can tendencies in that direction be ignored.

The argument that the effective role of the state is limited because it cannot be capital has also been put on the grounds that state activity is unproductive. A total state capital is therefore an economic impossibility within capitalism. Despite the often abstruse manner in which this type of argument is put, it has little real force. It is clear that a large part of state activity is unproductive in the sense that it supports the production of surplus value but does not itself produce it. But this does not apply to the whole of the state's activity. Nationalised industries produce surplus value in exactly the same way as do private concerns. The difference in legal ownership does not affect the relations of production. The fact that profit records are often low or even negative is neither here nor there since surplus value must not be confused with book profits, and complex mechanisms exist to redistribute surplus value within capitalism. Indeed what distinguishes the state from private enterprise is not that one fails to produce surplus value while the other does, but that in the state the various mechanisms by which surplus value is redistributed are far more complex than in the private sector.[28]

In fact these arguments, although they are more sophisticated than those of Hilferding, lead their supporters into much the same kind of dilemma. They all set limits to capitalism which the system itself has an unfortunate habit of transcending. In Hilferding's case he solved the problem by denying capitalism itself; now the problem is resolved by denying the state the role it can be shown to have in modern capitalism. Any limits set in this way must be arbitrary and the past history of capitalism does not augur well for any argument which dogmatically ignores the flexibility of the system and its ability to absorb new forms.

A Final Reformulation

In Bukharin's early presentation of his theory of state capitalism by far the weakest aspect was his tendency to suggest that it would result in the rational organisation of the national economy. This was something he referred to on a number of occasions. A typical statement is his comment that 'capitalist "national economy" has moved from an *irrational* system to a *rational* organisation.'[29] Critics have been quick to pick this up, understanding by it that he foresaw a situation in which the state could overcome its internal contradictions. Lenin, too, in his marginal notes to *The Economics of the Transition Period*, seems to have interpreted Bukharin in this light.[30] It seems clear, however, that there is no basis for this. Bukharin was referring not to some form of extra-system irrationality in the sense of a Hilferding or a Bauer, but a specifically capitalist rationality. Nevertheless, the failure to explore the internal contradictions of state capitalism can still be counted as a serious gap in his argument. However, from the mid-1920s he began to reformulate the theory of state capitalism and take the argument one step further. This is the importance of two articles he wrote on modern capitalism in 1929.[31]

In these he argued that far from bringing a generalised rationality to capitalism as a system, the various tendencies towards state capitalism were creating what he called 'the economics of organised chaos'. He began by reviewing the work of various western economists on what Sombart termed 'late capitalism'. These, he argued, all neglected the role of the world economy and the ways in which the dying-out of competition at home led to its intensification abroad. Up to this point he merely restated his old argument. But he went further. To the extent that capital becomes centralised, he argued, so does the market come to play less and less of a role. The various organisational links in the economy become ends in themselves:

> the market can bring pressure to bear on them only through a number of intermediate stages. The pressure of reality (in this case the market) loses its original force and does not introduce the necessary corrections where they are needed.

In this situation the capitalist economy becomes a bureaucratic economy.

Bukharin was well aware of the work of Max Weber, but he went beyond him in trying to show the specific way in which bureaucracy derived from the forms that were created by the expansion of value in late capitalism. It was not a disembodied social phenomenon but a direct product of capitalism as a mode of production. 'Bureaucratisation of the economy is the fate of capitalism,' he wrote, and it leads to a general 'economic arteriosclerosis'.

He then identified what he saw as the major contradictions which affect the internal workings of the increasingly state capitalist economies of modern capitalism. One is the difficulty of economic calculation. As the market disappears internally and as it is imposed externally in a highly mediated form, so economic calculation becomes more and more difficult. It becomes necessary to search for appropriate organisational forms which can yield a degree of rationality and replace the disciplining force of market competition. But in such situations the ideas of 'rationality' and 'optimality' are indeterminate. When means become ends and human beings are subordinated to the machine, how is the machine to be run? Who, indeed, is to run it? What is now necessary is a new emphasis on the selection of personnel and on the quality of management and this leads to an even more detailed control of social life.

These were tendencies and problems that Bukharin saw around him and they were reflected in a major change in bourgeois ideology away from that based on the *rentier* and which he had analysed in his youth,[32] to that of the organiser, the manager who faced new problems and new tasks under late capitalism.

The development of his argument along these lines gave considerably more coherence to his whole case for state capitalism. Unfortunately, it came too late for him to have time to develop it in full. Elements of these themes can be found in his various writings on fascism in the 1930s, but what we are left with is essentially a suggestive picture of the internal condition of a modern statified capitalism.

In more modern terms we can reformulate Bukharin's argument along the following lines: as the state intervenes it faces two problems which serve only to intensify the difficulties to which its intervention was a response. In the first place, the state finds it impossible to achieve a rational restructuring of capital towards areas of highest profitability both because it needs the output of the weaker units of capital to serve the state capital as a whole and because it is denied a direct means of evaluating relative profitability. (In terms of conventional economics it cannot solve the problem of allocative efficiency in production.) In the second place, the efficiency of the extraction of surplus value at the point of production also suffers as bureaucracy stifles control over the process of production. Costs cannot be minimised and output maximised. This latter problem of non-allocative efficiency at the point of production was subsequently rediscovered by conventional economics in the 1960s and labelled 'x-inefficiency'. Interestingly, the term was used both to distinguish the problem from that of allocative efficiency and because x represents the unknown, reflecting the difficulty that neoclassical economics has in dealing with this problem. One feels that Bukharin would have appreciated the irony of this belated recognition of a problem he had identified some 40 years before.

One promising way in which Bukharin could have taken these arguments further would have been to relate them more closely to his analysis of the theory of crisis and capitalist dynamics. In his book on *Imperialism and the Accumulation of Capital* he posed the question of whether accumulation is possible in a state capitalist economy, and he answered in the affirmative. But, he added, there would be 'no crisis of overproduction' since the state as capitalist could now match supply and demand. Such an argument, however, did not follow from his premises. To sustain it he would have to assume no foreign trade, or total control over the foreign trade sector. But both these assumptions are illegitimate (except in the short run) in the light of his general analysis of the world economy. In this sense, although under state capitalism the state has more power to moderate crises of overproduction, they will still exist as a result of the participation in the world economy. Moreover, Bukharin then went on to another illegitimate argument arguing that the dynamic of a state capitalist system would be sluggish on the grounds that 'the capitalists' consumption constitutes the incentive for production and the plan of production. Hence, there is no *particularly* fast development of production (small number of capitalists).'[33]

The problem here is that the rate of accumulation is not determined by the capitalists' consumption, but by the competitive, expansive dynamic of the system as a whole. This was something that Bukharin had demonstrated elsewhere − the imperative to accumulate is a product of the anarchy of capitalist competition. This would still exist in a world economy of state capitals. From this perspective accumulation only slows to the extent that the rate of profit falls but, as we have seen, this was a line of investigation that Bukharin did not pursue. Had he done so he could have rounded off his analysis by including state capitalism in the 'unity of contradictions' which create capitalist crisis. Here state capitalism would appear as both an effect of the crisis and a further cause. It is precipitated as a response to falls in the rate of profit, but because of 'the economics of organised chaos' that Bukharin described it offers no guarantee that this can be resolved. On the contrary, the risk is that a fall in the rate of profit will be perpetuated and intensified as a result of the inability to force through a thorough restructuring of capital with the result that state capitalism must lean heavily upon repression and holding down consumption for its survival.

In this respect aspects of what Bukharin might have called the 'pure model' could certainly have been better formulated but the analysis of the tendencies towards state capitalism that he described still constitute a point of departure for an understanding of the modern world. Marxists ignore it at their peril. The ageing of capitalism in the years since Bukharin's death has entailed no let-up in the processes he described. The trend towards a greater role for the state has been a common one. Its crudest measure is the rise in state expenditure as a share of total output. A more significant measure is the direct role of the state in accumulation either through its ownership of state capital or its support of private capital. As a trend this has gone furthest in the weakest sectors of the world economy — the ramshackle economies of the Third World, and the faltering industrial economies of Europe, like those of Britain and Italy — but it shows no sign of abating anywhere. Periodic attempts are made to roll back and restructure the state, in Bukharin's terms to transfer control and ownership back into the 'private' pocket of the ruling class, but their effect has been in the area of reducing the 'burden of welfare'. The price of labour is cheapened, while the state, as capital, marches on.

State and Revolution

Bukharin continued to develop his analysis of the capitalist state throughout his life, but the political conclusions of the analysis were obvious from the time that he first outlined it in 1915 and 1916. Far from socialism being the advance of the state and state property, its first act would be the destruction of the existing bourgeois state and its replacement by a qualitatively new form. In this way Bukharin became the first Bolshevik to recapture the full sense of Marx's argument that the working class could not simply lay hold of the existing state. In Bukharin's war-influenced imagery, it was necessary to 'blow up' the capitalist state if the transition to socialism was to begin.

When he put this argument he was immediately accused by his opponents in the socialist movement of 'peddling' 'anarchist fairy-tales'. His response was to argue that the nature of capitalism and the capitalist state itself determined the nature of its overcoming. Capitalism tied the class form and the class content of the state in such a way that they could not be separated. Since the state was the main organisation of the bourgeoisie then it followed that to defeat the bourgeoisie it was necessary to defeat its state as well. Indeed, he went further and, anticipating later theories of 'dual power', he argued from the experience of 1905 in Russia that 'the Soviets of Workers' Deputies in Russia were an embryonic form of proletarian state power. But they were able to appear only because of the colossal disorganisation of the Tsarist governmental apparatus.'[34]

But this 'colossal disorganisation' had to be encouraged not only to defeat the bourgeoisie as a social force. The state was both a political relation and a social relation, he argued. In its latter form its overthrow was also necessary if the social rule of capital was to be overcome. It is

here that he began to turn his analysis of state capitalism into the beginnings of an analysis of the transition to socialism. Because the capitalist
state is both a product of capital as a social relation and acts to per-
petuate it and even to carry that relation in a very extreme form, so
here too the destruction of capitalism demands the destruction of the
capitalist state as its first act.

In 1916 and 1917 these arguments were relatively weakly developed
but they were sufficient to set Bukharin sharply at odds with many on
the Left, including Lenin. From their respective exiles in Scandinavia
and Switzerland they began a debate which covered not only the state
but also the national question where Bukharin and his Left supporters
took a position close to Rosa Luxemburg and refused to support
slogans for 'national self-determination' in favour of what they saw as a
higher internationalism. But the hostility spilled over into each area.
For Lenin, Bukharin had become '(1) gullible to gossip and (2) devilishly
unstable in politics'. His hostility to the state was 'either supremely
inexact or incorrect'.[35] The vituperative nature of the debate, more on
Lenin's side than Bukharin's, was later to provide choice material for
Stalin's historians seeking to show the irreconcilable differences that
had always divided Bukharin from Lenin. Relations, according to
Shlyapnikov who acted as a bemused 'buffer' between them, did
indeed become 'extremely strained. Contacts with and work for Russia
were the first to suffer, and these for me counted above all else.'[36]

A number of things lay behind the intensity of this clash. The first,
as Shlyapnikov noted, was a general tendency on the Russian Left to
pursue disagreements to their bitter end; 'this phenomenon is . . .
endemic in our intelligentsia which is so doctrinaire in defence of its
"principles" that it will even abandon the work in hand.' This tendency
was then accentuated by the conditions of relative isolation in exile.
'Lack of activity oppressed Bukharin,' reports Shlyapnikov, and we
know that the same applied to Lenin.[37] Then, more seriously, we must
remember the catastrophic impact that the collapse of the European
Left in 1914 had on those who remained loyal to the idea of international socialism. Where once differences had been ignored or papered
over, it now seemed necessary to expose them lest they led to more
serious divergences. This seemed particularly necessary in Russia where
there was a larger and more amorphous bloc of socialists (including
some in the Bolshevik Party) holding a position between open support
for the war and open opposition to it.

But there was also a fourth and more fundamental factor at work
here. This was the uneven and semiconscious way in which Lenin,

Bukharin and other Russian revolutionaries were breaking with the old Marxism of the Second International. Intellectual breaks are rarely clean and this was true of both Bukharin and Lenin. The most basic rupture had been made by Lenin in 1914 in his *Philosophical Notebooks* where he went back to Hegel to reject the mechanical determinism of the Second International and to recognise the depth of Marx's perception of socialism as the self-emancipation of the working class. Bukharin never made this philosophical break with the same clarity and cogency as Lenin, as is evident from his later discussions in his *Historical Materialism*.[38] But in his analysis of the state he leapt ahead of Lenin whose arguments developed much more slowly. As late as December 1916 Lenin was writing that Bukharin's argument was 'entirely muddled. It is un-Marxist and unsocialist'. But the muddle was more on Lenin's side, as Bukharin later noted:

> Il'ich ... did not take the correct position on the 'explosion' of the state (the bourgeois state, of course), confusing this question with the withering away of the dictatorship of the proletariat. Perhaps I should have further developed the theme of the dictatorship at this time. But in my defence I can say that *at that time* there was such indiscriminate Social-Democratic glorification of the bourgeois state that it was natural to concentrate all attention on the question of the explosion of this machine.[39]

In this half-light the debate confused serious points and errors on both sides with 'pettiness'. In the end, the Petersburg Committee of the Bolshevik Central Committee was asked to look at the various differences and, while supporting Lenin in principle, it effectively rebuked him and his collaborators in Switzerland for the handling of the disputes.

> the Bureau finds that the divergences between the contributors and the editorial board of the central organ [*Social-Democratic Notebook*] on particular questions of the minimum programme must not form an obstacle to the participation of these individuals in the Central Committee publications.[40]

Lenin, however, had already determined to respond more substantially to Bukharin, and in 1917 he began to work on the analysis of the state. The question of state capitalism was not a real issue between them. Lenin's original comments had been that Bukharin's arguments

were 'interesting' and Lenin was to use the term himself interchange-
ably and unselfconsciously with 'state monopoly capitalism' when in
the future he discussed capitalism. His aim was rather to show the
error of Bukharin's insistence on the conclusion that the capitalist state
would have to be smashed in a socialist revolution. But the theoretical
volte-face was to be his own. By February and March 1917 he was busy
filling out the notebooks that would provide the basis for *State and
Revolution* which he was to write that summer, and in the process he
quickly came to see the substance of Bukharin's argument and its
foundation in Marx and Engels' own analyses. 'Revolution,' he was to
write in *State and Revolution*, 'consists not in the new class commanding, governing with the aid of the *old* state machine, but in this class
smashing this machine and commanding, governing with the aid of a
new machine.'[41] When Bukharin returned to Russia in the spring of
1917 from an exile that had taken him across Europe to the United
States, Lenin was still in hiding. But he soon met Lenin's wife,
Krupskaya, and he later recalled that her first words to him were that,
'V.I. asked me to tell you that he no longer has any disagreements with
you on the question of the state.'[42]

Then in October 1917 the question ceased to be a theoretical one.
Revolution in Russia threw the Bolsheviks into power and the problem
now became how to develop an analysis of the transition to socialism.
That analysis would have to grow out of the analysis of the nature of
capitalism. 'The society of the future will not be conjured out of a
void,' Bukharin wrote, 'nor will it be brought by a heavenly angel. It
will arise out of the old society, out of the relations created by the
gigantic apparatus of finance capital.'[43] As we have seen, Bukharin, in
analysing these relations, had emphasised first, that capitalism was a
world economy and that, secondly, it was driven within this world
economy towards forms of state capitalism. The building of the new
society would therefore have to involve a negation of both these
aspects. The question was how was this to be done?

Notes

1. G. Hardach, D. Karras and B. Fine, *A Short History of Socialist Economic
Thought*, London: Edward Arnold, 1978, p. 46.
2. N.I. Bukharin, *The Economics of the Transformation Period*, New York:
Bergman, 1971 (hereafter *Economics*), p. 224; N.I. Bukharin, *Imperialism and
the World Economy*, London: Merlin, 1972 (hereafter *World Economy*), pp.
9-14.

3. Quoted in Hardach, Karras and Fine, *op. cit.*, p. 55: see also H. James, 'Rudolf Hilferding and the Application of the Political Economy of the Second International', *The Historical Journal*, vol. 42, no. 4, 1981, pp. 847-69.

4. Quoted in M. Croan, 'Prospects for the Soviet Dictatorship: Otto Bauer', in L. Labedz (ed.), *Revisionism*, Allen & Unwin, 1962, p. 289.

5. C. Buci-Glucksman, *Gramsci and the State*, London: Lawrence & Wishart, 1980, part 3.

6. M. Sawyer, 'The Genesis of "State and Revolution" ', in R. Miliband and J. Saville (eds), *Socialist Register 1977*, London: Merlin, 1977, pp. 213-18.

7. N.I. Bukharin, 'Gosudarstvennyi kapitalizm i markizm', *Novyi Mir* (New York), no. 848, 2 December 1916, pp. 4, 6.

8. Ibid.; N.I. Bukharin, 'Toward a Theory of the Imperialist State' (1916), in N.I. Bukharin, *Selected Writings on the State and the Transition to Socialism*, Nottingham: Spokesman, 1982, *passim*.

9. N.I. Bukharin, 'Contradictions of Modern Capitalism', *The Communist Review*, vol. v, no. 7, 1924, pp. 321-5.

10. Hardach, Karras and Fine, *op. cit.*, chapters 3, 4 *passim*.

11. See R. Day, *The 'Crisis' and the 'Crash': Soviet Studies of the West 1917-1939*, London: New Left Books, 1981, for the Soviet discussion.

12. Although Bukharin mentions the falling rate of profit in a number of works his most extended discussion is in N.I. Bukharin, 'Marx's Teaching and its Historical Importance', in N.I. Bukharin *et al.*, *Marxism and Modern Thought*, London: Routledge, 1936, pp. 60-2.

13. See his comments in *Economics*; and D. Maretskii, 'Nikolai Ivanovich Bukharin', *Bol'shaya sovetskaya entsiklopediya*, 1st edn, vol. viii, Moscow, 1926, p. 276.

14. 'Gosudarstvennyi kapitalizm', *op. cit.*

15. *World Economy*, p. 63.

16. 'Toward a theory', *op. cit.*

17. Ibid., pp. 13-14, 16-17.

18. On the changes in the first world war, see G. Hardach, *The First World War 1914-1918*, London: Allen Lane, 1977.

19. *World Economy*, p. 158.

20. *International Press Correspondence*, vol. 8, no. 1, 5 January 1928, pp. 30-1.

21. *Economics*, pp. 21, 19.

22. *World Economy*, p. 157; N.I. Bukharin, *Historical Materialism – A System of Sociology*, New York: International Publishers, 1925, p. 252.

23. Ibid., pp. 153-4.

24. *Economics*, p. 29.

25. For a discussion of Gramsci's analysis in these terms, see Buci-Glucksman, *op. cit.*

26. R. Hilferding, 'State Capitalism or Totalitarian State Economy?' reprinted in R.V. Daniels (ed.), *The Stalin Revolution*, Boston: D.C. Heath, 1965, pp. 94-7.

27. J. Habermas, *Legitimation Crisis*, London: Heinemann, 1976, p. 47.

28. R. Compton and J. Gubbay, *Economy and Class Structure*, London: Macmillan, 1977, chapters 5 and 6.

29. *Economics*, p. 19. L13, L15a.

30. Ibid., L13, L15a.

31. N.I. Bukharin, 'Nekotorye problemy sovremennogo kapitalizma u teoretikov burzhuazii', and 'Teoriya "organizovannoi bezkhozyaistvennosti"', in *'Organizovannyi kapitalizm'*, Moscow: Communist Academy, 1930. The latter is translated as 'The Theory of "Organised Economic Disorder"', in N.I. Bukharin, *Selected Writings on the State and the Transition to Socialism*, Nottingham:

Spokesman, 1982.

32. N.I. Bukharin, *The Economic Theory of the Leisure Class*, New York: Monthly Review Press, 1972.

33. R. Luxemburg and N.I. Bukharin, *Imperialism and the Accumulation of Capital*, London: Allen Lane, 1972, p. 226.

34. 'Gosudarstvennyi kapitalizm', *op. cit.*, p. 4.

35. Some of the basic documents of these debates can be found in O.H. Gankin and H.H. Fisher, *The Bolsheviks and the World War*, Stanford: Hoover Institution, 1940, pp. 213-56. For a commentary on the debate so far as it related to the state, see Sawyer, *op. cit.*

36. A. Shlyapnikov, *On the Eve of 1917*, London: Alison & Busby, 1982, p. 113. Shlyapnikov's account of this period, written in the 1920s, is invaluable both for its information and its relative freedom from later factional issues. In this sense it contains more genuine memoir material and a better 'feel' of the time than later accounts. See L.E. Holmes, 'Soviet Rewriting of 1917: The Case of A.G. Shlyapnikov', *Slavic Review*, vol. 38, no. 2, June 1979.

37. Shlyapnikov, *op. cit.*, pp. 113, 121.

38. Bukharin's book on *Historical Materialism* was intended as a popular textbook. The most famous and substantial critique of it was by Gramsci, A. Gramsci, *Selections from the Prison Notebooks*, London: Lawrence & Wishart, 1971, pp. 419-72. It was also attacked by Karl Korsch and Georg Luckács. These critiques were parts of attempts to overcome the limitations of Second International Marxism, but the book also had its critics in Russia, albeit from a different direction. Bukharin's reply to the latter is available in French as an appendix to N.I. Bukharin, *La Théorie du Materialisme Historique*, Paris: Editions Anthropos, 1967, pp. 340-50. It should be added that Second International Marxism was by no means as crude as it has often been portrayed, nor was Bukharin's book (especially given its popular nature), but the defects were real and serious and were no doubt some of problems that led Lenin to make his famous comment on Bukharin in his 'Testament' (see Chapter 6).

39. Bukharin made these comments in 1925 when his seminal article on the theory of the imperialist state was first published, N.I. Bukharin, *Selected Writings on the State*, *op. cit.*, p. 33.

40. Shlyapnikov, *op. cit.*, p. 201. The Petersburg Committee with Shlyapnikov at its centre was to move quickly to support Lenin's *April Theses*. It is interesting to note in the light of this resolution recorded by Shlyapnikov that Stalinist historians in 1931, seeking to equate Lenin to Stalin to legitimise the latter, condemned Shlyapnikov's histories for showing Lenin only as a helpful comrade and not as 'the chief [Vozhd'] whose every directive had to be followed'!, quoted in Holmes, *op. cit.*, p. 241.

41. These notebooks are available in Lenin's collected works, and as *Marxism on the State*, Moscow, Progress, 1972.

42. N.I. Bukharin, *Selected Writings on the State*, *op. cit.*, p. 33.

43. N.I. Bukharin, 'Anarchy and Scientific Communism' (1918), in N.I. Bukharin, L. Fabri and R. Rocker, *The Poverty of Statism*, Sanday Orkney: Cienfuegos Press, 1981, p. 3.

4 TOWARDS A POLITICAL ECONOMY OF THE TRANSITION PERIOD: REVOLUTION AND CIVIL WAR

As we have seen, the form of the transition to socialism had not been widely discussed prior to the October Revolution. In this situation it fell to Bukharin to begin to develop a general analysis of both the nature of the revolution and the transition period. Much attention has been focused on one aspect of this — the debates over economic policy in the 1920s. Since the technical details of these debates are well documented there is little that can be added here.[1] What is important is to set the debates in their more general political context because this is something that few writers have done. In particular Bukharin's own policies were not derived out of the air but arose directly from his previous analysis of capitalism. Here we shall analyse Bukharin's position in two stages. The first ran from 1917 through the civil war to the inauguration of the New Economic Policy (NEP) in the early 1920s. The second stage begins with Bukharin's re-evaluation of his ideas after 1921 as the Russian Revolution failed to ignite Western Europe as the Bolsheviks had hoped it would. In these changed conditions Bukharin was forced to modify his analysis. This division is not unusual. However, unlike other accounts which picture his rethinking during NEP as involving a sharp break with his past analysis, we shall argue that it involved a working-out of his earlier position in the new circumstances of the time. In this sense it carried forward both the strengths and weaknesses of his earlier analysis, though these are not necessarily those that the conventional accounts recognise. In particular, we shall insist that Bukharin's analysis can only be understood on the basis of the Marxism that he espoused throughout his life.

It is this Marxism which is often played down in much of the current writing about Bukharin. Yet as we shall see, although in the 1920s the apparent unanimity of the Bolsheviks in the earlier years of the Revolution broke down behind the differences, there were still important shared assumptions. The differences that developed, for instance, between Bukharin and Trotsky should not obscure a wide area of agreement between them on some of the general lessons to be learnt from the Russian Revolution. The essence of these was summed up in a pamphlet Bukharin wrote in 1918:

much had already been written of the dictatorship of the proletariat, but no one knew exactly in what form it would be realised. The Russian Revolution shows us the precise form of that dictatorship. It is the Republic of Soviets. That is why the arms of the Soviets are inscribed on the banners of the best ranks of the international proletariat.[2]

When differences arose in the 1920s they were not over this issue. So far as the situation in Russia was concerned, they related specifically to the question of how a rapidly degenerating revolutionary state, left high and dry by the failure of international revolution, could begin to develop what Bukharin called 'a half-beggared country'. But before we can explore this we must first see how Bukharin drew out a general picture of the transition to socialism in the early years of the revolution.

The Russian Revolution and International Revolution

Bukharin saw the Russian Revolution as a general confirmation of the analysis of capitalism that he had developed in the previous three and a half years of world war. It was, he argued, a part of the general crisis of the capitalist world economy which had been precipitated by the war. It could only be appreciated, therefore, if one first understood the general dynamics of capitalism as a world economy. Here, however, Bukharin was less successful in relating his general analysis to the particular conditions in Russia. His weaknesses here were not so apparent at the time, but they were to create important problems in his analysis in the future.

In his preface to the first volume of *Capital*, Marx wrote that 'the country that is more developed industrially only shows, to the less developed, the image of its own future.'[3] In fact, Marx was far less sanguine about the possibilities of capitalist development than passages like this would suggest. In his various writings on colonialism, for example, he identified some of the ways in which the expansion of capitalism created vastly uneven structures of development and under-development, though without ever attempting to offer a theory of underdevelopment. Nevertheless, there is a general optimism in his writings about the possibilities of capitalist development and it was this that was picked up by the mainstream of the Second International and generalised into an argument about the stages of social development. It was this perspective that denied to Russia (a country where capitalism had yet to 'mature') the possibility of a socialist revolution in the immediate future. Rather, any revolutionary upheaval would be a bourgeois-democratic one, in which the working class and the peasantry would push a reluctant bourgeoisie to fulfil its historical mission of developing capitalism.

This was the position that Lenin rejected in his famous *April Theses* in 1917. Far from Russia having to wait on the further development of capitalism, it was the development of capitalism internationally that had forced the country to the forefront of the revolutionary struggle: Russia was the weakest link in the capitalist chain in the advanced world; capitalism had reached a point where it could go no further, where it could not mature and ripen; it was already over-ripe and it was the failure to develop Russia more that was the sign of this. As a result the Russian Revolution would be socialist and provide the clarion call for the European socialist revolution. In 1917 no-one put this position more forcibly than Bukharin. He had come to it before his return from exile after the February Revolution and in advance of Lenin's *Theses*. When he finally reached Moscow in May 1917 he immediately took up the argument for revolution, campaigning for it not only outside the Bolsheviks but also within the Party against more conservative sections which were particularly strong in Moscow.[4]

The particular logic of this position has long been associated with the theory of permanent revolution which Trotsky first developed after the failure of the 1905 Revolution. Bukharin's internationalism in 1917 has often been taken as evidence of the Bolsheviks' implicit support for this position at the time of the Revolution. But Bukharin's argument had important nuances which it is necessary to unravel because they have substantial implications for how he developed his analysis in the 1920s, and how he came to oppose Trotsky and the theory with which he is mistakenly associated in 1917. In order to see the logic of Bukharin's argument it is first necessary to summarise briefly Trotsky's own discussion of permanent revolution.

In fact Trotsky only fully developed his analysis of permanent revolution in the late 1920s and early 1930s under the influence of his reassessment of the Chinese Revolution of 1927;[5] the core of the theory, however, remained the same from the time of its first formulation after the 1905 Revolution.[6] Starting from the argument that capitalism is a world economy, Trotsky suggested that it could only develop its parts unevenly. Development in Russia combined pre-capitalist forms, particularly in the countryside, with the most advanced capitalist forms. This was what he termed 'uneven and combined' development as a result of which he saw capitalism creating a whole series of contradictions which prevented its further development. This he was later to generalise to undeveloped countries as a whole. The social consequence of this distorted development was that a distorted class structure had developed in Russia with a small and weak bourgeoisie that was afraid to take on the old classes for fear of encouraging the working class to revolt. This left the working class as the only progressive force capable of leading the revolution which, with the aid of the peasantry, would inevitably become a socialist revolution combining socialist and democratic demands. This revolution would then catapult the working class into power, but because of economic backwardness the conditions for the development of socialism would not exist. Therefore the revolutionary state had immediately to throw its weight behind international revolution to break out of its isolation and so make the revolution both international and permanent. This is a bold summary of Trotsky's position but it will be sufficient to show the way in which Bukharin converged with and diverged from this analysis during and after 1917.

Bukharin shared the two most important political conclusions of Trotsky's analysis – that the Russian Revolution would be socialist and that its success (and indeed survival) depended upon its becoming international. From 1917 to the early 1920s he distinguished himself by the strength of his desire to throw the full weight of the revolution behind international revolution. Indeed, unlike Lenin, he even used the term permanent revolution. In a pamphlet of 1918, for example, he argued that the revolution was being forced outwards in such a way that

> the problem of international revolution is posed more sharply than ever. . . . Thus the *permanent revolution* in Russia is transformed into a European revolution of the proletariat, armed by this same imperialist state over whose head the gleaming blade of the guillotine is already raised.[7]

Three years later the argument was no less insistent: 'The revolution can only win if it is world-wide. We have repeated this a thousand times. It is, thus, a necessity for us to take up any possibility of hastening the collapse of capital in other countries.'[8] But when one investigates the analysis that lies behind these conclusions it quickly becomes apparent that they were arrived at by a different route from Trotsky's. The result of this was that when Bukharin sharply diverged from

Trotsky in the 1920s it was less a betrayal of his earlier views than a working-out of a different logic already implicit in his position in 1917.

Bukharin's argument began from the same premise as Trotsky's — that capitalism had to be analysed as a world economy. Indeed, as we have seen, Bukharin not only accepted this but explored it in great detail. The first difference arose, however, over the weight to be placed on the uneven development of capitalism. Here, Bukharin's discussion lacked the sensitivity that characterised Trotsky's analysis of the contradictions of backwardness in general and Russian backwardness in particular. Bukharin had a cruder and more optimistic vision of the possibilities of capitalist development, which he set out generally in his book on *The World Economy and Imperialism*. There he drew a picture of a world economy which seemed to imply that it could even out differences in levels of development. He placed great emphasis on what turned out to be a temporary move in the terms of trade in favour of primary producers prior to the first world war and argued that 'we have entered an era of an accelerated industrialisation of agrarian countries.'[9] He then applied this specifically to Russia, suggesting that under the influence of both a rise in grain prices and agrarian reform there had been an accelerated development of capitalism in the Russian countryside.[10] In general terms this was true, but Bukharin analysed the process in such a way that the peculiarly uneven character of Russian development received less emphasis than it should have. In this way his analysis of rural relations lacked both the depth of that made by Lenin and Trotsky and was less in the centre of his analysis than it was in theirs.

In contrast to both of them, Bukharin put far more weight upon the influence of the world economy. The first world war, he argued, was a manifestation of an insoluble crisis in capitalism which showed that the world economy as a whole was ripe for socialism. It was this ripeness which made international revolution both possible and necessary. Russia fitted into this perspective in three ways. In the first place, the war had forced the development of state capitalism in Russia with the result that the more backward sections of Russian capitalism had been integrated with the more advanced, and a general levelling-up in development had occurred. This was certainly true of large parts of Russian industry but Bukharin also used the argument to slide over the backwardness of the countryside. 'As long as the state system of state capitalist organisation *as a whole* was strong, agriculture was also adapted to the *universal* apparatus, the main component of which was organised industry.'[11] Thus, because of its relation to the state, particularly through state control of distribution, Bukharin arrived at the conclusion that in spite of the low level of the productive forces in agriculture it was ripe for revolution.

On its own this somewhat forced argument would not have been enough to sustain support for international revolution, but Bukharin then implied it was all rather by the way since capitalism could not survive the war crisis in any case. There was therefore no choice but to go forward to socialism. This argument reflects the weakest aspect of Bukharin's Marxism at that time; what has been called by some writers his economism.[12] There is some truth in this charge. What Bukharin tended to do when he was discussing the prospects for revolution was to deduce particular political actions in a direct and mechanistic way from his economic analysis. He had already shown a lack of sensitivity to social and political factors in his disagreements with Lenin over the national question. Here he had argued that since national solutions to the crisis of capitalism were impossible it was wrong for revolutionaries to take up the national question and to support 'reactionary claims' for national self-determination. This was 'first of all *utopian* (it cannot be realised within the limits of capitalism) and *harmful* as a slogan which *disseminates* illusions.'[13] This argument appalled Lenin; not least because it was made at a time when practical connections were already being made between the fight for national independence and the fight for socialism at both ends of Europe — in Ireland and Russia. These had to be welcomed, argued Lenin, not because struggles for national self-determination were sufficient in themselves but because they were 'one of the bacilli, which help the real anti-imperialist force, the socialist proletariat, to make its appearance on the scene.'[14] But this element of economism was no less present in Bukharin's analysis of revolution in Russia though it called forth less sharp comments from Lenin. Again, Bukharin made the same jump from economics to politics by arguing that the international situation could only be resolved by international revolution and justifying the Russian Revolution as the 'torch ... [which] has fallen into the powder keg of the old, blooded Europe. It is not dead. It lives. It will grow. And it will merge inevitably with the huge triumphal uprising of the *world proletariat*.'[15] This leap becomes particularly clear in Bukharin's book *The Economics of the Transition Period* published towards the end of the civil war, and it was commented on a number of times by Lenin in his marginal notes. When Bukharin, for example, wrote that 'all concrete facts indicate that the elements of decay revolutionary dissolution of relationships advance with every month', he was corrected by Lenin who insisted that between economic 'decay' and 'revolutionary dissolution' the class struggle has to intervene![16]

Finally, Bukharin also advanced the argument that international revolution having taken place, it would then be possible to call upon the advanced technique of Western Europe to overcome Russian backwardness.[17] This formulation was less close to Trotsky's than it might at first sight seem, for Bukharin did not use it as a prominent argument for international revolution. Rather he took it as an axiomatic consequence of an international revolution whose logic was built upon a significantly different analysis from that offered by Trotsky. In short, whereas Trotsky's formulation of permanent revolution, whilst starting from the world economy, pushed the emphasis onto the way in which the internal contradictions within Russia would force the Revolution outwards to survive, Bukharin placed his emphasis on the way in which the Russian Revolution would be pulled outwards by the general crisis of capitalism of which it was a part. In this sense, in spite of his use of the term 'permanent revolution', he shared only some of Trotsky's conclusions in 1917 — not his argument.

The significance of this difference was not to become apparent until the early 1920s when Bukharin was forced by the failure of international revolution to reconsider his position. Capitalism, he would argue, had achieved a 'temporary stabilisation'. Thus one of the props of his earlier support for international revolution was removed. At the same time he also tried to rectify his political analysis and remove the economistic elements for which he had been attacked. This removed another prop of his support for international revolution — there was no insoluble crisis of capitalism and no inevitable revolution to flow from it. If, therefore, the Russian Revolution had to be an international revolution it would be necessary for him to recast his analysis. This was certainly possible but Bukharin was to be pulled in a different direction towards support for the proposition that Russia, in spite of its backwardness, could begin to develop its own socialism.

The Dictatorship of the Proletariat

Bukharin also saw the development of the Russian Revolution as a confirmation of his analysis in another sense. When he had first advanced his analysis of state capitalism and drawn the conclusion from it that socialism necessarily meant the destruction of the capitalist state itself in favour of a qualitatively new form which would arise from below — the dictatorship of the proletariat — Bukharin had drawn fire not only from Lenin but others in the social-democratic movement. Now he argued that theoretical debates were being resolved in action. He no longer had to argue for the need to smash the state for, he wrote triumphantly in October 1917, the Russian Revolution was itself showing that 'it is perfectly obvious that with the transition of power to the soviets the bourgeois state collapses.'[18] The problem was now no longer that of capitalism but the emergence of socialism.

Here Bukharin was concerned with revolution, not simply as an act of destruction of the old order but as an act of construction. Out of the elements of the old organisations, blown apart by revolution, the dictatorship of the proletariat had to be built. This was not to be identified with the creation of socialism but it was its prerequisite. Through the dictatorship of the proletariat the transition to socialism could be made, but this transition would require — and here Bukharin frequently quoted Marx — 'the inevitability of an entire *historical* period, the specific characteristics of which will distinguish it from both the capitalist period and the communist period with its rationally constructed stateless society.'[19]

The first question that this poses is, in what sense is the dictatorship of the proletariat distinct? For Bukharin the answer lies in the fact that it is not a 'form of government' but 'a new and distinctive *type of state*' — a state organisation of the working class. Its originality here is threefold. First, unlike previous states, the dictatorship of the proletariat represents the interests of the vast majority against a small number of exploiters. Secondly, it can represent this majority because it rests upon a new class base — the working class — whose control of it is founded in new, organic, institutional forms of which the Soviet is the most important. Thirdly, it is a temporary state in the process of dissolution for, to the extent that it is successful, it begins to wither away. This is not something that exists as a distant goal but as an immediate prospect.[20]

The problem of the nature of this new form of state was posed concretely in terms of its organisation. In reconstituting the elements of a state, 'the working class, which has seized state power, must inevitably become the power which appears as *organiser* of production.' The dictatorship of the proletariat was what Bukharin described as a direct class state where power arose directly from class organisation. It was both a *workers' state* and a *working state* in which the working class both determined decisions and carried them out. Workers' organisations were therefore an organic part of both the *government* and the *state*.[21]

The foundation of this new democracy is working-class political activity. This is reflected in the shift away from certain formal free-doms to a real democratic foundation in terms of the capacity to dis-cuss and determine policy. The essence of this democracy lay in a conscious and politicised working class which, through the state, could set the conditions which would maintain and develop its new role. A concrete expression of this idea was Lenin's wish to give 'equal right for public groups of a certain size (say, numbering 10,000) to a fair share of newspaper stocks and a corresponding quantity of printers' labour.'[22]

This conception of the dictatorship of the proletariat raises the question of its relationship to formal parliamentary structures. Before the October Revolution it had been the Left who had pushed for the convocation of a Constituent Assembly to lay the foundations for a genuine parliamentary form. The Bolsheviks had argued that the equi-vocations of the Provisional Government on this issue showed its undemocratic leanings. There was no coherent conception of how the Constituent Assembly would fit in with the new structure of revolu-tionary power but neither was there a clear awareness that it would be in contradiction with it. Indeed the early decrees of the Bolsheviks make explicit reference to the future of the Constituent Assembly.

Bukharin shared these ambiguities and, in his words, could be found 'trumpeting about getting the Constituent Assembly convened' no less than other Bolsheviks. But the fundamental question that the Constituent Assembly raised was that of the nature of power. By December 1917 he was arguing that the Left part of the Assembly should declare itself a revolutionary convention rather than a simple parliament – and presumably in this way still coexist in some form with the soviets. But even this proved unrealistic. The problem was partly that the election results gave the towns to the Bolsheviks but the countryside to the socialist revolutionaries. The vote for the latter was also confused by splits which had been obscured by a single united election list drawn up before the Revolution. But the fundamental problem was the real polarisation of power behind these results. As Bukharin insisted in his speech to the Assembly, power was now in the hands of class organs of workers, peasants and soldiers. The Constituent Assembly, however, represented another power as a supposed 'general', 'national' forum involving different classes. On the central issues such as the nature of the regulation of industry, control of the banks, the land, labour discipline, peace, etc. it had pull in a different direction with a different class character. This was recognised by the remnants of the old ruling class even if the socialist revolutionary leaders could not see it, and this was why the Assembly became a rallying point of opposition to the Revolution of those who had vacillated over its calling and even openly opposed it. In this more pragmatic fashion the Bolsheviks and Bukharin came to share the more general view that it was the soviets and not parliamentary forms that were 'the most perfect form of the dictatorship of the proletariat discovered by the Russian Revolution'.[23]

Here Bukharin found himself the major propagandist against those on the Left who still held to a parliamentary road to socialism, through the takeover of the existing state. Bukharin directed his arguments against two views of parliament. Against the middle-of-the-road social-democrats who believed in the possibility of parliamentary reform, he maintained that not only could it not bring socialism but that parliament itself was increasingly a charade. As state power increased so it was withdrawn from parliamentary control. To use the terminology first introduced by the English constitutional theorist, Walter Bagehot, there is a further shift between the *dignified* and *efficient* parts of the constitution. Whereas once parliament had been the working, efficient part, now it became part of the dignified structure, preserved in order to maintain allegiance to the real centres of power that now lay outside the control of any elected body. The real power lay, Bukharin argued, with the state apparatus itself and with increasingly detached executives at the head of it. Capitalism itself was dispensing with parliamentary forms except as a façade, 'a talking shop'. Moreover, such a talking shop depended for its credibility on the acceptance of a series of ideological fictions like those of the 'nation', 'community', 'commonwealth'; that is, precisely those fictions that class conflict breaks apart.[24]

But he also had to deal with a more sophisticated argument put forward initially by Karl Kautsky and taken up by various Austro-Marxists. This recognised that parliamentary government had little real power and served to obscure class realities. But it denied that this prevented parliament from being transformed into an institution of real power. This was the role of revolution. Thus Kautsky could write that 'parliamentarism, far from making a revolution useless and superfluous, is itself in need of a revolution to vivify it.'[25] But, if this is so, then Bukharin put the obvious reply. How, he asked, 'is it possible, in an age of civil war, to organise the proletariat in the forms of the old bourgeois democracy, which have been destroyed everywhere by finance capital?' If the development of capitalism itself destroys the power of parliament, and revolution destroys the fiction of the 'unity' of society on which the parliamentary form depends, then it is simply anachronistic to believe that the bourgeois parliamentary form can have a long life under socialism. Real social unity can only be created with 'the complete and decisive victory' of the working class, and not just nationally, 'its *world-wide* victory will ultimately restore the unity on a new basis, that of declassing society altogether.'[26]

In the meantime the problem was for the new, revolutionary state to survive at all in conditions of acute social polarisation and civil war. It was the character of this immediate problem that determined the nature of the tasks of the dictatorship of the proletariat and the way in which it would be able to meet them. It was to an elaboration of this that Bukharin now turned.

The Tasks of the Dictatorship of the Proletariat

First amongst the problems faced by the dictatorship of the proletariat was the continued opposition of the old order. This arose not just from internal forces but from the hostility of international capitalism. It was this, Bukharin argued, that gave confidence to the defeated internal bourgeoisie to continue their fight. As the reaction intensified in Russia and the civil war developed, Bukharin argued that the Revolution had to become an 'iron dictatorship' of the working class. Of course the term 'dictatorship' did not carry the connotations that it was later to be given, but Bukharin was prepared to see wide limitations on democracy. Such limitations, though, were distinct from those under capitalism in that they arose from a state that was itself the product of the working class. They were not imposed, he argued, over the working class but through it. They reflected what he hoped would be its organised self-discipline as a politically conscious class.

The defence of the Revolution against its enemies was, however, only the first of the tasks of the dictatorship of the proletariat. It was also, according to Bukharin, a necessary lever in the transformation of society. 'The new class, now in power, makes use of its power as a lever for economic upheaval, breaks up the production relations of the old type and begins to erect new relations.'[27] Its role here arises from what he saw as the very different nature of the transition from capitalism to socialism compared with the earlier transition from feudalism to capitalism.

Bukharin spent a considerable time exploring the basis of this difference. He argued that capitalist relations of production had begun to emerge out of the decline of feudalism long before bourgeois revolutions altered the political forms of the old order.[28] It was the well-established social power of capital that later enabled the bourgeoisie to consolidate its political power. In this sense bourgeois revolution was one of the last steps in the emergence of capitalism not one of the first. By contrast socialism simply cannot grow up within the womb of capitalist society. Only its material preconditions can develop there. Socialism must be preceded by a political revolution as its first act because only such a revolution can lay the basis for a conscious transformation of society and so allow the creation of new socialist relations of production. Thus the workers' state has to battle through time to build the new society. The bourgeoisie, Bukharin wrote,

> did not build capitalism, it built itself. The proletariat will build socialism as an organised system, as an organised collective subject. While the process of the creation of capitalism was spontaneous, the process of building communism is to a significant degree a conscious, i.e. organised process.

The working class acts as a conscious subject 'to break the old relations of production in the sphere of social economics'. Whereas under capitalism and state capitalism the political form is dominated by the economic, in the transition to socialism the world is turned upside down and the political now dominates the economic allowing a conscious suppression of the old by the new.[29] Here again Bukharin's argument reflects his earlier stress on the relationship between class forms and class content. Because the dictatorship of the proletariat is a lever of transformation it cannot exist over and above the working class but only through it. This, necessarily, puts a narrow limit on the variety of forms that a workers' state can assume. Such a limit is not apparent under capitalism because the power of capital is based upon its existence as a social force and it can therefore rule through a variety of state forms. The working class can only rule politically and this depends upon its direct control. (One consequence of this is that attempts to understand later developments in the Soviet Union in terms of some extended analogy with the 'autonomy' of the state under capitalism are grotesquely irrelevant.) Paraphrasing Marx, Bukharin wrote that 'the structure of society changes *through* men and not outside men. ... The new class, in this process, serves as the organiser and bearer of the new social and economic order.'[30] In this way the working class not only changes society, it also changes itself. It 'must *actively build up* socialism in this period and simultaneously, in the process of this rebuilding, re-educate itself.' It was because Bukharin saw this as a real possibility that he was able to contest the arguments of those like Weber, Pareto and Michels who saw bureaucracy, élites and oligarchies as universal forms in modern society. All of these theorists, Bukharin argued, pictured the 'incompetence of the masses' as a constant feature of history. Not seeing that this would be transformed, they were unable to see beyond the social and political forms appropriate to capitalism.[31]

It is important to stress at this point the emphasis in Bukharin's analysis on the role of the working class as the conscious subject of history. What it shows is that the common charge of 'statism' that is made against him, particularly in the light of his arguments in *The Economics of the Transformation Period*, misses the point. As the civil war progressed, the necessity for increasing discipline and coercion rose too but Bukharin insisted that it was a 'self-discipline' of 'the proletariat, as organised collective subject'.[32] Nor is this a distortion of what initially happened. As one historian has written, 'it remains difficult to explain the huge rise in the Party's numerical strength in 1918 ... if there was not at the very least a widespread acceptance, however unenthusiastic, of the need for order and cohesion.'[33]

In the light of later events it is easy to ignore the immediate circumstances and to counterpose democracy to centralism and to build into the obvious tension that exists between them a theory of the inevitable development of the revolution towards some authoritarian ending. This has been a constant theme of western historiography and it has mirrored the Soviet mythology that the Bolsheviks were from the outset a tightly disciplined party. Fortunately this view has been subject to growing criticism in recent years.[34] Suffice it to say here, in respect of the civil war period, that the problem of democracy and centralism was not seen in these terms at the time. One interesting manifestation of this was the way in which one of the earliest opposition groups within the post-revolutionary Bolshevik Party — the Democratic Centralists — demanded, in the midst of the civil war, both more democracy and more centralism![35]

The central problem was not the unravelling of some grand historical clash between two conflicting and abstract principles but the more down-to-earth and perhaps more tragic manner in which the civil war forced a pattern of development on the Bolsheviks that in the end no-one could control. It is difficult to exaggerate the impact of the civil war in throwing the Revolution off the rails. Just to keep going it was necessary to shift the whole of society onto a war footing as, faced from the summer of 1918 by better equipped armies supported by the western powers, the revolution was forced to defend itself to the death. At one point three-quarters of Soviet territory was occupied and the military situation was so desparate that munitions were being taken from the Tula arms factories to be used on the front the same day that they were produced. The impact on the economy was devastating. During the worst period the Bolsheviks held only 10 per cent of coal supplies, 25 per cent of the iron foundries and less than 50 per cent of the grain area of the old Russian Empire. In the face of this, economic and urban decline quickly followed. Instead of being able to expand the output available to society at large the Bolsheviks were faced with a dramatic cycle of what Bukharin called 'negative reproduction'. The new society was not even reproducing itself – it had been forced into a cycle of decay. The Bolsheviks reacted to this in the only manner possible, namely, by more and more centralisation. This was the only way in which each shortfall in production and distribution could be dealt with in the midst of war. The Revolution had to be defended and they had their backs to the wall.

The problem was that these were not simply economic changes. The civil war had equally dramatic effects on the class base of the regime. In fact it went a considerable way towards destroying the working class as a class. As a result the whole base of the new state was cut away. What Bukharin had seen as the 'organised collective subject' had begun to disappear by late 1918 and early 1919 as a result of death and privation. It was as a product of this war-induced social crisis that discipline and coercion ceased in any meaningful sense to be of the working class, by the working class and through the working class. The working class was no longer there, it was at the front or back in the countryside scavenging for food, or dead in an unmarked grave.

The tragic irony of this situation for the Bolsheviks was later well caught by Victor Serge:

we have conquered everything and everything has slipped from our grasp. We have conquered bread and there is famine. We have declared peace to a war-weary world, and war has moved into every house. We have proclaimed the liberation of men, and we need prisons, an 'iron' discipline – yes, to pour our human weakness into a brazen mould in order to accomplish what is perhaps beyond our strength – and we are the bringers of dictatorship. We have proclaimed fraternity, but it is 'fraternity and death' in reality. We have founded the Republic of Labour, and the factories are dying, grass is growing in their yards. We wanted each to give according to his strength and each to receive according to his needs; and here we are, privileged in the middle of generalised misery, since we are less hungry than others.[36]

It is said that when the civil war ended, on average some 17 cartloads of filth were taken from every house in Moscow. Piles of excrement, cholera and typhoid were no basis for a leap into the realm of freedom. The problem was that given that this disaster had occurred how were the Bolsheviks to react? Bukharin's own weakness, we shall argue, lay in the particular way in which he failed to respond sufficiently to the processes of degeneration within the new state itself that these tragic events had set in motion.

'The Economics of the Transition Period'

In *The Economics of the Transition Period*, which he wrote while the civil war raged, Bukharin mapped out a four-stage model of what he meant by the transformation of relations of production. This was a model of revolution drawn from the work of a fellow Bolshevik economist, Kritsman. The first stage of the model was that of the ideological awakening — the working class, within capitalism, begins to become conscious of its power. This is then followed by the second stage of political revolution when the working class actually takes power. The third stage is then one of economic change as 'capitalist relations of production are smashed'. Finally the transition is completed in the fourth stage of technological revolution, when a new 'rationalised social technology' is developed.[37]

In discussing this model Bukharin stressed that these stages were not immutable. They could overlap, and this was especially so in the case of the third and fourth stages. Nevertheless, the approach is schematic and it is passages like this that have led some writers to claim that the early Bolsheviks had the same narrow view of transforming relations of production that came to characterise Stalin's analysis in the 1930s. This latter view tended to see both relations of production as being a technical problem and to reduce changing them to a simple matter of economic development.[38]

This view highlights a real weakness of certain aspects of Bolshevism that Bukharin shared. The very backwardness of Russia led to an emphasis on the advantages of modern technology and even, in some instances, towards a support for western forms of scientific management like Taylorism. As a result the Bolsheviks paid little attention to exploring the nature of the labour process and this undoubtedly contributed to the tendency to slide over the question of the real situation of workers in the 1920s. In this sense the contrast with the focus of much modern Marxist theory is striking. But it is dangerously misleading to equate this lack of appreciation of the nature of technology with the positive approval that it was later given under Stalin. Nor is it correct to read back the argument that relations of production would change simply as a consequence of economic development. To see this it is necessary to examine how Bukharin came in practice to give some life to the abstract view of the transition that he borrowed from Kritsman, and this entails an examination of the economics of the transition period as he saw them in this early period of revolution and civil war.

Understanding Bukharin's analysis of the transition period is complicated by three factors. The first is the intrinsic difficulty presented by the period itself. This was well expressed by Bukharin in the chapter of *The Economics of the Transition Period* that he wrote with Pyatakov. There he remarked that, 'in the very period of transition the categories of being must, for very obvious reasons, be replaced by categories of becoming.'[39] This makes the problem of fetishism and the relation of content and form particularly difficult to analyse. Secondly, Bukharin himself complicated matters by not always clearly distinguishing between his discussion of the immediate situation and the final triumph of communism. His *Economics of the Transition Period* must be particularly carefully read with this distinction in mind. Thirdly, there is the need to distinguish those elements which he saw as specific to the Russian situation, whether in the form of war communism or the later NEP, and those elements which he saw as the essence of any transition. If these latter points are borne in mind, then Bukharin, even in his most 'Left' phase, appears as much less extreme than many commentators have drawn him.

These qualifications are important because the basic conception of the transition to socialism held by all of the Bolsheviks in these years was heavily influenced by the experience of 'war communism'. As Bukharin later wrote,

> we thought that our peacetime organisation of work, our economic policy, the building of our economy would be a further continuation of the centralisation of planning of this time ... for us war communist thought was not 'bound by the war' ... but a universal, general and, so to speak, 'normal' form of economic policy of a victorious proletariat.[40]

But it would be wrong to conclude from this that the nature of the attachment to war communist methods among different Bolsheviks was all of a piece. Once the NEP had been introduced and Bukharin had become convinced of its necessity, viability and 'normality', he hammered away at the continued influence of war communist 'illusions' in the Party, suggesting in the process that he had followed these 'illusions' to their extreme. With NEP had come their collapse or 'liquidation',

> this does not at all mean that the war communist system was incorrect in its fundamentals for this time. In conditions of internal and external blockade we were forced to act in the way we did. But that is just the point, we did not see all of the relativeness of war communist politics.[41]

But this was to overstate his own attitude to war communism at the time. If we examine his arguments then, it is clear that although the 'universal illusions' that he later condemned abound, they are by no means as great as in the case of other Bolsheviks, nor were they developed to the same extremes. Moreover, there is a clear perception that war communism was not simply a leap towards full communism. It can be argued that it was more theorists like Kritsman (at the economic level) and Trotsky (at the political level) who were more totally carried away by war communism. Certainly Bukharin did not shrink from the need to use force and militarisation in the midst of a civil war (though he remained convinced that it was qualitatively different from the force and militarisation equally in evidence on the other side) and in the particular and well-known instance on the debate on the role of the trade unions at the end of 1920 he had followed Trotsky in supporting state control of unions rather than Lenin, who argued that they had a role to play in protecting workers against 'a workers' state with a bureaucratic twist to it'.[42] But it is difficult to see in the light of his general analysis that he could have given the same blunt and unqualified celebration of the 'state' that Trotsky did:

> Just as a lamp before going out, shoots up in a brilliant flame, so the State, before disappearing, assumes the form of the dictatorship of the proletariat, *i.e.* the most ruthless form of State, which embraces the life of the citizens authoritatively in every direction.[43]

Moreover, while Bukharin, like Trotsky, was to justify in the new conditions of the 1920s the continuing *in principle* of pragmatic moves made against opposition outside and inside the Party in the civil war (even while they both suffered from them), unlike Trotsky he was prepared to make much greater modifications of his views in other ways which suggests that his war communist 'illusions' had shallower roots.

Bukharin's initial thinking about the economics of the transition was conditioned by his confidence in international revolution. This, as we have seen, sprang less from a theorised vision of permanent revolution than his belief in an insoluble world crisis. Because of this the issue of socialism in one country did not arise, nor did the question of sustained accumulation. This can be seen in the absence of a discussion of these problems in his work before 1921. In *The Economics of the Transition Period*, for instance, he is concerned with three issues. The first is the way in which revolution necessarily leads to a decline in the productive forces and the consequences this has. The second is the various social forms that arise when the working class 'builds as class subject, as organised power'. Then thirdly, there is the question of the way in which the forces of production are *restored*. It was only later, with the coming of NEP, that he was forced to take up the issue of accumulation and its relation to the theory of socialism in one country.

Bukharin argued that revolution necessarily involves a decline in the productive forces, a process of 'negative reproduction' or disaccumulation. As he later put it, 'the use of telegraph poles for barricades will not encourage the increase in production.'[44] He was well aware that the extent of the decline in Russia was a consequence of its specific situation, but he still held that the principle of decline was a general one. At the level of both production and institutions, the working-class seizure of power involves a 'colossal disorganisation' which brings a period of temporary chaos during which new forms are established. These difficulties are increased by the necessity to win over key groups like the old intelligentsia to the side of the working class. Bukharin did not expect that this problem would be easily solved anywhere. Beyond this there is also the problem, implicit in the fact of revolution as a process of self-organisation and self-transformation of the working class, of the need to fight for the establishment of a new collective self-discipline. He had no illusions that there was anything automatic in this.

The new relationships would be reflected in organisational forms which centralised power on a new class basis. At this level, 'the dictatorship of the proletariat will formally have similarity with the epoch of the dictatorship of the bourgeoisie, i.e. will be state capitalism turned upside down, its dialectical reversal of poles into its own opposite.' This dialectical negation is created by the way in which the new state is now based on the working class itself. The working class 'builds its apparatus, the base of which is made up of the *workers' organisations*'. The organised working class therefore provides the basis of the new state and the framework which allows it to be reconstituted to incorporate, in a subordinate position, elements of the old structure. The image Bukharin uses here is that of working-class organisations constituting a 'web' into which elements of the old forms are integrated.[45]

What makes it difficult to analyse further Bukharin's conception of the transition at this time are the emergency measures forced by war communism. In both *The Economics of the Transition Period* and *The ABC of Communism* Bukharin emphasised that they gave the dictatorship of the proletariat a military character that it otherwise would not have. This has been neglected by those who have tried to construct a continuity between Bolshevik ideas at this time and the consolidation of Stalinism in the period of the first Five-Year Plan. Arguing that war communism was a form of 'analogue' of later events, they have accused Bukharin in particular of being led astray at this time and in this way paving the way for later events.[46]

Bukharin certainly saw elements of the economics of war communism as a step towards socialism, but even at its height he ridiculed any suggestion that it was anything near to a finished form as 'an absurd barbarism' and he looked forward to a respite from its rigours for the serious task of reconstruction. Indeed, it is significant that to sustain the argument that Bukharin saw in the measures of war communism 'a direct transition to communism' one of the major proponents of this, Charles Bettelheim, is forced to truncate his quotes, removing Bukharin's qualification that the form of working-class administration of industry in the civil war has been 'adapted to the relations of quick working, to the "pace of war"', and ignoring his emphasis on 'proletarian-militarized production'.[47]

But the whole direction of the argument also needs to be contested not least, as Ralph Miliband has stressed, 'as a matter of simple historical accuracy'. We can do no better than quote his judgement here since it applies as much to Bukharin as to the Bolsheviks as a whole.

The notion that there is anything remotely analogous between the experience of war communism and Stalinism is a gross perversion of the truth. Much that was damaging was done in those early years . . . and some of it is directly attributable to Lenin. But there is nothing in the period in which Lenin was at the head of the Revolution which begins to resemble the later experience. . . . Obviously, the centralisation of power which occurred and the 'military style' which came to dominate the way things were done were of help to Stalin in his ascent to power. But to make too much of this is to blur . . . the fact that it took a qualitatively different state of affairs to make possible the 'liquidation' and incarceration of millions upon millions of people, the creation of an all-pervasive police regime based upon fear and delation, the total suppression of any vestige of criticism of Stalin and his policies.[48]

Notes

1. See A. Erlich, *The Soviet Industrialisation Debate, 1924-1928*, Cambridge, Mass.: Harvard University Press, 1961; P.R. Gregory and R.C. Stuart, *Soviet Economic Structure and Performance*, New York: Harper & Row, 2nd edn, 1981, chapter 3.

2. N.I. Bukharin, *Soviets or Parliaments*, London: Workers' Socialist Federation, 1920, p. 4.

3. K. Marx, *Capital*, vol. 1, Harmondsworth, Middlesex: Penguin Books, 1975, p. 91.

4. S. Cohen, *Bukharin and the Bolshevik Revolution*, Oxford: Oxford University Press, 1980, pp. 49-53. Although based solely on Petrograd, D.A. Longley, 'The Divisions in the Bolshevik Party in March 1917', *Soviet Studies*, vol. 22, no. 1, July 1973, pp. 61-76, shows that the early divisions in 1917 were more complex than is normally allowed.

5. L. Trotsky, *Leon Trotsky on China*, New York: Monad, 1976.

6. For a discussion of the evolution of Trotsky's theory, see Jean-Jacques Marie, 'La révolution en Russie chez Léon Trotsky', in Fondation Giangiacomo Feltrinelli, *Histoire du Marxisme Comtemporain*, Paris: Union Générale d'Éditions, 1979, pp. 11-55.

7. N.I. Bukharin, *De la Dictature de l'Imperialisme a la Dictature du Proletariat*, Geneva: Edition Universa, 1918, p. 6 (my emphasis).

8. N.I. Bukharin, 'De la tactique offensive', *Bulletin Communiste*, vol. 2, no. 14, 7 April 1921, p. 220.

9. N.I. Bukharin, *Imperialism and the World Economy*, London: Merlin, 1972, pp. 90, 159.

10. N.I. Bukharin, *Na podstupakh k oktyabryu*, Moscow and Leningrad, 1926, pp. 19-28.

11. N.I. Bukharin, *The Economics of the Transformation Period*, New York: Bergman, 1971 (hereafter *Economics*), p. 86.

12. C. Salmon, *Le Rêve Mathématique de Nicolai Boukharine*, Paris: Le Sycomore, 1980.

13. O.H. Gankin and H.H. Fisher, *The Bolsheviks and the World War*, Stanford: Hoover Institution, 1940, pp. 213-36.

14. Quoted in T. Cliff, *Lenin*, vol. 2, London: Pluto Press, 1976, p. 55.

15. N.I. Bukharin, *De la Dictature, op. cit.*, p. 72. In this perspective, of course, the military attacks on the fledgling socialist state were a confirmation of the links between the Russian and world revolutions. As Bukharin said in the Central Committee debates on the Treaty of Brest-Litovsk, 'events have developed *as they had to*. There are signs of panic and bewilderment here. We foresaw

everything that is happening now. We said that either the Russian Revolution would spread or it would perish under the pressure of imperialism' (my emphasis). *The Bolsheviks and the October Revolution. Minutes of the Central Committee of the Russian Social-Democratic Labour Party (Bolsheviks) August 1917-February 1918*, London: Pluto Press, 1974, p. 208.

16. *Economics*, pp. 54, 214; see also Lenin's notes against the passages numbered 37, 39, 45 for other examples.

17. N.I. Bukharin, *Na podstupakh k oktyabryu, op. cit.*, pp. 146-7.

18. Ibid., p. 144.

19. N.I. Bukharin, 'The Theory of the Dictatorship of the Proletariat' (1919), (hereafter 'The Theory'), in N.I. Bukharin, *The Economics and Politics of the Transition Period*, London: Routledge & Kegan Paul, 1979, p. 36. *Economics*, chapters 7-8.

20. 'The Theory', *op. cit.*

21. *Economics*, p. 79; 'The Theory', *op. cit.*

22. V.I. Lenin, *Collected Works*, 4th edn, vol. 26, Moscow: Progress Press, 1972, p. 283.

23. *The Bolsheviks and the October Revolution, op. cit.*, pp. 154-6; 'Rech' na pervom zasedanii uchreditel'nogo sobraniya', in *Na podstupakh k oktyabryu, op. cit.*, pp. 178-80; 'The Theory', p. 51.

24. Ibid., pp. 41-7.

25. K. Kautsky, *The Social Revolution*, London: Twentieth-Century Press, 1909.

26. 'The Theory', pp. 41-3.

27. N.I. Bukharin, *Historical Materialism. A System of Sociology*, New York: International Publishers (1921), 1925, p. 259.

28. Bukharin's most developed expression of this is only available in Russian, 'Burzhuaznaya revolyutsiya i revolyutsiya proletarskaya' (1922), in N.I. Bukharin, *Ataka*, Moscow, 1924.

29. *Economics*, pp. 68, 71.

30. *Historical Materialism, op. cit.*, p. 308.

31. *Economics*, p. 68; *Historical Materialism, op. cit.*, pp. 309-10.

32. *Economics*, pp. 128, 151, 156.

33. R. Service, *The Bolshevik Party in Revolution*, London: Macmillan, 1979, p. 91.

34. S. Cohen, 'Bolshevism and Stalinism', in R.C. Tucker (ed.), *Stalinism: Essays in Historical Interpretation*, New York: Norton, 1977.

35. Service, *op. cit.*, p. 108.

36. V. Serge, *The Conquered City*, London: Gollancz, 1975, pp. 30-1.

37. *Economics*, pp. 70-1; *Historical Materialism, op. cit.*, pp. 255-62.

38. See, for example, Salmon, *op. cit.*

39. *Economics*, p. 134.

40. N.I. Bukharin, 'O likvidatorstve nashikh idei' (1924), in N.I. Bukharin, *Put' k sotsializmu v Rossii: izbranniye proizvedeniya*, New York: 1967, p. 178.

41. Ibid.

42. On Bukharin's role here, see S. Cohen, *Bukharin and the Bolshevik Revolution, op. cit.*, pp. 102-6. Bukharin's position, it should be stressed, was not identical with Trotsky's.

43. L. Trotsky, *Terrorism and Communism* (1920), Ann Arbor: Ann Arbor Paperbacks, 1969, p. 109. For an able discussion of the problems in Trotsky's analysis of this time which does not see them simply as proof of the 'totalitarian soul' of Bolshevism, see J. Molyneux, *Leon Trotsky's Theory of Revolution*, Brighton: Harvester Press, 1981, pp. 66-83.

44. *International Press Correspondence*, vol. 4, no. 50, 25 July 1924, p. 510;

Economics, chapters 3-4, 6.

45. Ibid., p. 76.

46. Salmon, *op. cit.*; C. Bettelheim, *Class Struggles in the USSR, First Period: 1917-1923*, Hassocks, Sussex; Harvester Press, 1977; L. Szamuely, *First Models of the Socialist Economic Systems*, Budapest: Akadémiai Kiadó, 1974.

47. Bettelheim, *op. cit.*, p. 158; *Economics*, pp. 127-9.

48. R. Miliband, 'Bettelheim and the Soviet Experience', *New Left Review*, no. 81, May-June 1975, p. 66.

5 TOWARDS A POLITICAL ECONOMY OF THE TRANSITION PERIOD: THE NEW ECONOMIC POLICY

The society that emerged from the civil war was very different from the one that had entered it. Industrial production had slumped to one-tenth of its 1913 level and to obtain this reduced output it had been necessary to adopt extreme methods of centralised organisation. Some 5000 one-man enterprises had been 'nationalised' and even the production of pens and pencils had been brought within the system of priority organisation by the state. Domestic trade had given way to widespread barter, and grain for the towns had been collected from the countryside with the aid of military force. But this forced requisitioning of grain had not been sufficient to maintain the size of the urban population. Those who were left in the towns at the end of the civil war saw themselves as threatened by the turmoil of the countryside and the possible mass revolt of the discontented peasants. Yet initially the momentum of wartime thinking pushed the Bolsheviks to continue the war-induced policies of war communism even though military action was being wound down. Far from this improving the situation it only served to intensify the social crisis and, pushed by Lenin, the Bolsheviks were forced to shift their ground radically and adopt the policies that became known as the New Economic Policy (NEP). In particular, this involved a step back from the highly centralised state control that had been adopted in the war towards a more market-based policy in the economy. But at the social level it also involved a general freeing of society in the early years as the threat of immediate military defeat ended.

Bukharin, like all of the Bolsheviks, was forced to adjust the position he had adopted during the civil war and in the process he began to extend his analysis of the transition to socialism. His early interpretation of the break with war communism was that it was a retreat: 'Nine-tenths of the New Economic Policy of Russia is due to the peasant character of the country, i.e. to specific Russian conditions,' he wrote in 1921.[1] Subsequently he came to generalise the principles of NEP as a method of transition for all peasant-based countries. But, contrary to what has often been said, this did not lead him away from revolution towards some kind of gradualism. He always remained clear that revolution was necessary to end the rule of capital. But the tasks of a working class that had conquered power, he argued, were very different from those of a working class still struggling for power.

The wider background to Bukharin's rethinking was set by the new situation that the Bolsheviks found themselves in. The failure of international revolution, and particularly the failure of the German revolution of 1923, profoundly affected both Bukharin and the mood of the Party as a whole. Once more the Revolution was thrown back on its own paltry resources. Bukharin now argued that it was essential for the Bolsheviks to consolidate their position at home and begin to rebuild Soviet society. The positive side of his argument was that it led him to think through how a relationship could be forged with the peasants in the countryside. This led him to a perception of the role of the peasantry and the nature of the rural situation which, we shall argue, was better than anything produced by his contemporaries and especially the Left. At the same time, however, his understanding of this aspect of the problems facing the new state was not matched by an equal development of his conception of the relationship of the Revolution to the outside world. Here a crucial break occurred which we argued in Chapter 4 was already implicit in his earlier analysis. Bukharin now moved away from his earlier support of international revolution to embrace the vision of 'socialism in one country'. The consequence of this was that he increasingly separated his analysis of the domestic situation in the 1920s from the external one, and as a result, pushed his analysis of world capitalism and the pressures that it created into the background as far as the transitional state was concerned.

The redirection of Bukharin's thought in these years has often been pictured as 'a violent about turn', both politically and theoretically – a shift from the far Left of the Bolsheviks to the extreme right wing. Certainly, until the end of the civil war Bukharin was, in his own words, 'always to the Left of the Party'.[2] But to suggest that he subsequently turned sharply to the Right is a doubly inadequate characterisation of his attempt to grapple with the nature of NEP. In the first place, such a view misses many essential aspects of continuity in his thought. In the second place, unless the polemic of the Left and Stalin's later attacks on Bukharin as part of the so-called 'Right opposition' are taken at face value, it is difficult to take seriously the idea that Bukharin represented a rightward-moving section of the Party, shifting as a result of the pressure of the wealthy peasants – the kulaks. Bukharin's position in the 1920s developed out of his earlier analysis and, in political terms, he came to define the centre ground of NEP politics, not the Right.

Yet what sustains this inadequate characterisation of Bukharin's position is the deep complexity and ambiguity of NEP politics and the way in which the battle-lines that were drawn then still continue to imprison and limit debate today. In fact, although it is not obvious from the violence with which the debate is still continued, no-one in the 1920s was entirely correct in their analysis. All sides were compromised to a greater or lesser extent by their failure to appreciate that the real threat to the extension of the Revolution would come from Stalin. And then, even when this was finally realised, no one at the time was able to supply more than hints as to the nature of his power. If, therefore, we are to understand the failure to make the transition to socialism in these years then the battle-lines must be rejected along with the political characterisations that flow from them. In particular, we must recognise that the various political stances of the time were not always substantiated by the theories on which they were supposedly based. For instance, it was to be Trotsky who was to prove the most resilient of Stalin's opponents and to him goes the distinction of carrying forward the Marxist tradition at a time when Stalinism almost succeeded in destroying it. But Trotsky's own analysis was deeply flawed, and this led him to a series of judgements (on the peasantry and Stalin for example), which, with the benefit of hindsight, seem grotesque. These misjudgements did not simply reflect Trotsky's lack of information, though at times this factor did seriously impede him in the 1930s;[3] they had deeper theoretical roots in Trotsky's own failure to understand the nature of the transition. In fact, we shall argue that it is within Bukharin's analysis that one finds the beginnings of an answer to the question of how things went wrong. But Bukharin too was unable, in practice, to develop these beginnings into a coherent theory, and in the end he became far more deeply compromised politically that Trotsky ever was. But this political failure should not be allowed to obscure the fact that his analysis of the transition, for all its faults, offered a better promise of understanding both the transition and the actual degeneration than the analysis put forward by the various oppositions and that developed by Trotsky in the 1930s.

We can see how necessary it is to break from the conventional battle-lines if we first examine the question of the relationship of the Russian Revolution to international revolution. This was the area where Bukharin got himself into the greatest difficulties but it was also the area where, potentially, his own theory could have led to very different conclusions.

Socialism in One Country or Permanent Revolution?

Of all the nationalisations that socialism has carried out, said the Italian socialist Ignazio Silone, by far the most successful has been the nationalisation of socialism itself. The full horror of this was apparent in the first world war when socialist fought socialist in the name of a higher patriotism. The Russian Revolution had stood out against this mutual slaughter with its call for an international socialist revolution. But in the 1920s the Bolshevik Party as a whole also began to retreat from this position towards the idea that it was possible to build socialism in one country. The theory of socialism in one country received its fullest development under Stalin as a legitimating device to justify the industrialisation drive and the repression that necessarily accompanied it. But it was Bukharin who, in the first instance, gave the theory a coherent formulation. As he developed it, the theory was never as firm as it was to become under Stalin, but Bukharin's role in the retreat from '1917' was considerable. How was this possible in view of his earlier position?

Bukharin's arguments about the possibility of building socialism in one country crystallised in his debates with Trotsky over the other major position of the time – that the Revolution could only survive if it was made international in the form of permanent revolution. Here Trotsky tried to distil what he saw as the lessons of the October Revolution and to apply them on an international scale. In fact, both sets of arguments that Bukharin and Trotsky put forward were rent by major contradictions and neither of them necessarily supported the political conclusions that they drew from them. To understand this it is necessary to begin to disentangle the strengths from the weaknesses of each side in the debate.

There are two grounds on which the possibility of socialism in one country can be denied. One is to argue that the economic and social contradictions of backwardness in a country like Russia prevent the movement forwards to socialism in the absence of support from abroad. The other is to argue that international capitalism, working through the pressure of the world economy, has such a corrosive effect that it will force an accommodation with the capitalist world economy (albeit perhaps in new institutional forms) unless the revolution moves outwards to break the pressures that threaten to imprison it.

Trotsky oscillated between these two positions without ever seriously developing the second and finally came down in favour of the first. His rejection of the possibility of socialism in one country came to rest, in the first place, on the way in which he saw the Revolution being besieged in the 1920s by the mass of the peasantry, with the wealthier kulaks carrying the seeds of a new capitalism and revolutionary degeneration. Secondly, he stressed the way in which Russia lacked the necessary accumulation of capital and technique to provide the basis for a development into socialism. Paradoxically though, he was led by his fear of the peasantry to argue for a faster rate of industrialisation in the short run to strengthen both the state sector and the social position of the working class. In the long run, however, the strength to solve the contradictions of the time and to hold back the kulaks could, he argued, only come from the success of international revolution.

This argument, even in its most sophisticated form, was far from satisfactory. It led Bukharin, first, to argue that Trotsky had misunderstood the situation in the countryside and underestimated the peasantry. Secondly, he argued that Trotsky had also underestimated the potential for continued development on the basis of Russian resources alone. That these were poor meant that development would be relatively slow but it did not mean that it could not take place. Indeed, Trotsky's own support of a faster rate of industrialisation than Bukharin himself wanted at crucial times in the 1920s cut the ground from his denial of 'Russian potential'.

With hindsight we can see that Trotsky's theory had other deficiencies too. It led directly to his misunderstanding of the nature of the degeneration of the Revolution. Because Trotsky saw the threat of degeneration arising in the countryside, as a result of the pressure of the kulaks, he failed to identify the growing challenge of Stalin and those around him.[4] Moreover, the theory also contained a logical flaw. It was supposed to demonstrate how the success of any revolution was indissolubly linked to its spread abroad. But if the root of the problem which cements the link is backwardness then socialism in one country ought to be possible in an advanced country. It might not be on the agenda in Russia, but it would seem to follow that it could be in, say, Britain or the United States.

Indeed, of course, the ambiguities of the theory were such that Trotsky even retreated in the 1930s on the question of Russia itself. Far from seeing Stalin's rise and the industrialisation drive as a total counter-revolution, he equivocated and identified the resulting society as what he called 'a degenerate workers' state'. By this he meant a state in which the workers had no real power but which was in some sense still developing on the basis of 1917. But if this was so, where did this leave his earlier denial of the possibility of such development occurring at all? One seems left with the conclusion that the problems are only superstructural — a conclusion he toyed with though rejected without putting anything substantial in its place. Perhaps in the light of this it is not surprising that those who attempted to make anything of Trotsky's analysis in Russia in the 1930s found to their dismay and consternation that the theoretical difficulties of his position and the political mis-judgements it entailed gave them little to hang on to.[5]

It is not surprising, then, that Bukharin rejected Trotsky's argument. But the question still remains, is it possible and necessary to reformulate the theory of permanent revolution or does the rejection of Trotsky's particular argument lead directly to the justification of socialism in one country? On the face of it, given Bukharin's earlier analysis of the nature of capitalism as a world economy, it would seem that Bukharin did have the basis of developing his own ideas towards an alternative formulation of the theory of permanent revolution along the second line that we have identified. In this case it would be not backwardness but the pressure of world capitalism that would force the revolution outwards or force it into an accommodation. But, as we saw in Chapter 4, Bukharin's earlier support for international revolution had not involved him in drawing out the theoretical implications of his analysis of capitalism as a world economy. The consequences of this were now to be felt for, rather than being led to follow through the logic of his analysis of capitalism as a world economy, Bukharin attempted to attach to it a theory which seemed to fly directly in the face of his earlier discussion. In so doing he rejected not only the particular arguments that Trotsky put forward but also the general position on the necessity of international revolution.

There are, no doubt, many reasons why Bukharin moved in this direction. Historians have commonly pointed both to the way in which the theory of socialism in one country met the needs of a weary population and the way in which it reflected the interests of the growing bureaucracy in NEP Russia. Theoretically, however, we can see how, once Bukharin had failed to extend his theory of capitalism as a world economy, socialism in one country followed logically from the weaknesses of his earlier discussion of the relationship of the Russian Revolution to international revolution. The main threat of armed defeat had been overcome, and in the 1920s capitalism managed to recover from the crisis that had followed the war. This relative and temporary stabilisation meant that in the short run the Soviet Union was not faced by direct military challenge.[6] He did not ignore entirely the other forms in which the world economy could exert a corrosive pressure, but he argued that these could be contained. The domination of the new state by the working class provided the real barrier to the world economy. Against the pressure of capitalism would be set the interests of the working class in consciously subordinating social production.

At the same time it was also possible, he argued, to build links with the peasantry at home so that the major internal threat disappeared as well. It was out of this that the possibilities of development arose. He did not open up a vision of rapid development. On the contrary, he stressed the painful nature of the process without aid from abroad. 'We shall proceed with our development *more slowly. All the same we will go forward without hesitation,*' he wrote,

> we have already demonstrated that we can build socialism without any direct technical economic aid from other countries. It is true that the forms of our socialism in the coming period of construction will inevitably be those of a backward socialism. But . . . these forms guarantee a continuing movement toward other forms of socialism, which are more full and complete.[7]

The result of all this was that Bukharin could no longer accept the argument that socialism in one country meant the sacrifice of international revolution to the national interests of the Soviet Union.[8] In fact, he argued the opposite, namely that the successes of the Soviet Union, however limited, would encourage revolution abroad. The really grim perspective was that of Trotsky and the opposition. If their arguments were followed then the Soviet Union would represent

> *only the torch* of the international revolution, only the *cry for help* of our proletariat, a torch which is already smouldering in the vapours of 'Thermidor'. . . . In this way the opposition's appeal to the international proletariat to join the international revolution is an appeal of *despair.*[9]

The success of building socialism in Russia would give the western working class renewed confidence and so act as a powerful lever to revolution. Hence there was no contradiction between the national aims of the Soviet Union and the international aims of the working class. Indeed, the Soviet Union 'must be protected to the last drop of blood . . . everything must be sacrificed, everything staked in order to protect this country at any price, whenever danger threatens it.'[10] In his own terms he was not betraying his earlier belief in international revolution, in the holy war of the proletariat he was an internationalist but one, unlike Trotsky, who had realistically adjusted to the new situation.

This was an argument that Bukharin put in good faith. He did not share the more cynical view of, say, Stalin and Rykov, that revolution abroad could be sacrificed to defend the national interests of the Soviet state and their own political interests.[11] But Bukharin's argument was naive and not the least because the Stalins and the Rykovs could hide behind it while they made franker appeals to the weariness and disillusionment with revolution of the growing bureaucracy. Moreover, Bukharin could only sustain the general tenor of his analysis, no matter what the merits of particular parts of his case, by an appeal to three giant assumptions which he portrayed as incontestable. The first was his assumption that the national interests of the Soviet Union and the international proletariat could *never* clash. The second was that this was guaranteed by the basically healthy state of the Party and its leadership. The third was that this healthy state was in turn protected by the absence of forces (other than the opposition) subverting the Revolution. Unfortunately, history was to show just how 'heoric' these assumptions were. The Revolution was rapidly degenerating. Far from there being a recovery from the set-back of the civil war the process of bureaucratisation continued apace: the cancer in the Party continued to grow. Consequently there was no guarantee that the national interests of the Soviet Union would not clash with the interests of international revolution.

In fact, some of the negative consequences of this degeneration were already apparent in 1923 before Bukharin had fully formulated his case. Permanent revolution did not involve a fatalistic waiting for revolution, but its active encouragement. Instead the Soviet leadership in the Communist International and Soviet diplomacy acted as at best passive factors and at worst negative ones as their influence spread from Europe into Asia. First, in 1923 in Bulgaria and then more spectacularly in Germany, then in 1924 in Estonia, in 1926 in Britain and in 1927 in Austria and more notably in China opportunities to capitalise on crises were missed. It was not necessarily that each of these cases presented clear chances of revolution though that was certainly true in Germany and China. What was important was the failure to realise any of their potential. The weaknesses and immaturities of the native communist parties combined with the weaknesses of Soviet policy, led to defeat and set-back and this then led into further caution and isolation in the Soviet Union. Compared with the fear that the

Revolution had inspired in the ruling classes of Europe between 1917 and 1921 it was now accommodation that seemed uppermost. Christian Rakovsky tried to insist on this for the opposition at the 15th Party Congress in December 1927. As a revolutionary who had been at the centre of Soviet diplomacy throughout the 1920s he now saw a 'tragic' situation where, for the first time since October 1917, the workers' state had 'ceased to be an ideological danger for the capitalist governments'.[12] The capitalist governments might not have been quite so sure, but Rakovsky's experienced judgement should have added weight to the sorry history of the failure of the Revolution to spread in the 1920s. But Bukharin had remained blind to the problem and Rakovsky, like Trotsky, was on the way out, denied a serious hearing.

Indeed as the fortunes of Trotsky and his supporters, of Zinoviev and Kamenev had all declined, Bukharin's had risen and he had come to occupy a leading position in the Communist International. It was from there that, notably in the Chinese Revolution, he became himself a vehicle of the growing gap between the aims of the Soviet leadership and international revolution.[13] Only in late 1927 and 1928 did he begin to get an inkling of the scale of the problems in the Soviet Union.

In the meantime, in domestic policy, he had been making a more positive mark by laying out a far more successful analysis of the *smychka* – the alliance between the workers and the peasants in the transition to socialism.

Accumulation and the Smychka

Internally the difficulty that the Bolsheviks now had to deal with under NEP was accumulation. To understand the significance of this it is important to recognise that this was not simply an economic issue. The problem was not one about rates of investment as such. The real question that was posed was whether sustained accumulation could occur without necessarily reproducing the social organisation and classes appropriate to it – namely, capitalist forms. Marx had argued that socialism presupposes the abundance of developed capitalism. In this sense the question of sustained accumulation did not arise for him. Capitalism would already have eliminated the need for this by developing the productive forces to a high level. Yet in Russia this did not exist. The Bolsheviks had, in Bukharin's phrase, plucked a green fruit. What had justified this was the expectation of international revolution because, taken as a whole, capitalism on a world scale was ripe for socialism. But now this world revolution was not forthcoming — at least in the immediate future — and Russia faced the problem of how it was to develop.

With hindsight we can pose the issue with more clarity than it was seen with at the time. No-one had expected to confront this problem and it is not surprising that the answers that were forthcoming were unsatisfactory. For some it was sufficient to attach the prefix 'socialist' to accumulation for the problem to be solved. Bukharin was not so simplistic. He attempted to develop a sophisticated analysis of the politics of accumulation in the transition in which he saw the country-side as a potential ally rather than a source of political threat in the form of pro-capitalist kulaks, as with the opposition and later Stalin. In this, we shall argue, he showed true insight into both the politics of the transition and the actual relations in the Russian countryside in the 1920s.

The core of Bukharin's analysis of NEP was the idea of the 'workers' and peasants' alliance'. This was not a definition of the state which remained for Bukharin (both in theory and practice) a workers' state.[14] What it expressed was the policy of the workers' state in leading the peasantry to socialism. For Bukharin this was the 'most essential and original feature of Leninism'. It was embodied in Lenin's rethinking in the years after 1921 and it received its clearest expression in his article, 'On Cooperation', written shortly before his death.[15] In taking up and developing this idea Bukharin claimed to be doing no more than mapping out Lenin's road. His major work of the mid-1920s, *The Road to Socialism and the Worker-Peasant Bloc* (1925), was, he claimed, only 'my outline of Lenin's ideas as he expounded them to me'.[16]

According to Bukharin's interpretation, 'Leninism contends that the peasantry is to be the ally of the working class during the whole transition period.' The possibility of this was reflected in the fact that, divorced from its connections with capital and the world market by the dictatorship of the proletariat, the 'laws of development of agriculture' do not remain the same 'under the rule of the proletariat as they were under capitalism'.[17] If the peasantry was an ally and not the embodiment of the threat of capitalist restoration then it was possible gradually to reform agriculture and for the peasantry to grow into socialism.

Much of Bukharin's argument can be understood in terms of the concept of hegemony. The workers' state had to win the support of the peasantry on a voluntary basis. To achieve this political goal it had to offer tangible economic benefits:

the peasantry's confidence in Soviet power can be achieved only to the extent that Soviet power proves capable of providing *economic* leadership for the entire country . . . if the reverse were to happen, then *a transfer of political influence over the peasantry from the proletariat to the bourgeoisie would prove to be completely unavoidable.*[18]

This was the argument that he set out in a number of articles in the 1920s and popularised in his book *The Road to Socialism and the Worker-Peasant Bloc*. Here he developed the basic set of ideas which he was to uphold both against the opposition and, when the collectivisation drive began, against Stalin.

Bukharin, then, sharply counterposed two paths of development. One was the path to disaster and the fall of Soviet power. This lay in breaking the alliance with the peasantry and it was this road, he argued, that the opposition was urging the Soviet state to take in the 1920s; and it was this road that was eventually taken by Stalin. The other path was the path to socialism and it lay in the development of the worker-peasant alliance.

To maintain the support of the peasantry Bukharin argued that the workers' state should give maximum support to the improvement of the peasant economy through the development of the cooperative movement.

What will take place is the *remaking* of farms, their transformation on a cooperative basis. The growing incomes, the growing rationalisation, etc., will simultaneously mean attracting these farms through *cooperation* into the general system of our economy, in which socialism is being built. We must aim not at the elimination of the peasant economy, but at *attracting* it into the system of the state economy.[19]

These cooperatives would develop in different ways that reflected the social structure in the countryside but they would be part of 'the links' in the 'chain of the socialist economy'. Supported by the state they would, through self-improvement, lead to the levelling-out of the differences between the town and the country. The town would cease to be 'a vampire' sucking the rural community dry as it was under capitalism. At the same time, within the countryside itself, exploitation would also come to an end. The basis of prosperity in the cooperatives would be the peasants' own efforts at improvement and not the exploitation of the rural poor as had occurred in Tsarist Russia. To the extent that wealthier peasant groups existed they would not become a real threat to Soviet power because on every side their development would be constrained by that power.

Above all Bukharin emphasised that the success of these cooperatives depended upon winning the voluntary support of the peasantry. The links in the chain of socialism would be forged when the dictatorship of the proletariat showed that it could consolidate the power of the cooperatives economically and win the peasants politically through the revived rural soviets. The coercion of the civil war had to give way to a genuine attempt to gain the peasants' confidence.

This was a perspective, moreover, which came to have a wider significance for Bukharin. On a world scale capitalism had developed an industrial core in only a limited geographical space. In this sense the problem of town and country in Russia was a microcosm of the world situation. He estimated that the Russian working class was no more than a tenth of the size of the peasant population of some 100 million grouped in over 20 million peasant farms. The world situation was similar. If the working class did not make the peasantry its ally more generally therefore, he saw the very possibility of socialism being denied. The implication of rejecting the idea of a worker-peasant alliance, he argued, was that socialism could only be carried out against the interests of the vast majority of the world's population – a conclusion which, of course, still retains its point today.[20]

Nevertheless, this analysis immediately clashed with that of the emerging opposition in the 1920s. They quickly came to see Bukharin's more favourable assessment of the peasantry as the promotion of a series of fatal compromises. What he was doing was playing into the hands of the kulaks. In the face of this what was necessary, claimed the opposition, were policies that would counter the kulak threat. These policies would involve a speeding-up of the tempo of industrial growth by squeezing the peasantry to secure the funds needed for accumulation. This would then lead both to the economic strengthening of the state sector against the countryside and its political strengthening through an increase in the social weight of the working class.

Bukharin's response to this attack was twofold. In the first place, he denied that it was possible to squeeze the peasantry to the extent that those like the economist Preobrazhensky advocated. The response of the peasants, he argued, would be to withhold their grain. This was precisely the type of measure that would stimulate the growth of the kulaks and force the poorer peasantry to rely on them. Far from strengthening the Revolution, the policies of the Left would lead to a crushing ideological and political defeat through their alienation of the peasantry. But secondly, he argued that the opposition's analysis also completely misrepresented conditions in the countryside and the nature of the peasantry. Bukharin did not deny that social differentiation existed in the Russian countryside but he did deny that it was proceeding at the alarming rate that the opposition, and later Stalin, suggested. In this there is little doubt that he was right. Unfortunately an appreciation of this has been obscured by the way in which Soviet history has become obscured by myth.

According to the traditional account the opposition's warnings about the kulaks proved justified after 1927 when grain was increasingly withheld from the towns. It was then left to Stalin to expropriate the policies of the Left and develop them to a degree that they could never have imagined, smashing peasant resistance through wholesale collectivisation. It was thus possible both to maintain control of the countryside and to generate a surplus for massive investment in industrialisation.

In fact, as Bukharin feared, Stalin's 'smashing of the kulaks' was the destruction of an imaginary class. At the time, even with the aid of distortions, economists could not show that the kulaks existed on any substantial scale. Subsequently, historians have had the same trouble in finding this 'class' — kulaks, it sees, are like God, a matter of faith and the lack of them bad faith. Class analysis did not determine policy. Rather, as E.H. Carr has put it, 'policy determined what form of class analysis was appropriate to the given situation.'[21]

Similarly, the vast grain reserves that were supposed to be held in the villages were never found. These were, as Bukharin claimed in his famous attack on Stalin made in 1928 in 'Notes of an Economist' simply 'fairy' or 'old wives' tales'.[22] The shortfall in grain marketed to the towns, which in any case was greatly exaggerated by Stalin, was due in reality to a mistaken policy which had given insufficient support to peasant self-improvement and, by offering prices for meat that were too high relative to grain, had encouraged the peasants to convert their grain into meat in the form of increased livestock production.

How much Stalin believed in the threat of the kulaks is a matter of debate. There is, however, good reason to believe that he deliberately manipulated the fear to his own advantage. What is not in doubt is the tragic way in which the Left opposition continued to delude itself about this 'danger from the Right' and to identify Bukharin with it. Chasing phantoms, they lost sight of the real threat of the growing power of Stalin. 'With Stalin against Bukharin? — Yes,' Trotsky had exclaimed. 'With Bukharin against Stalin? — Never.' Only too late did he realise the blunder he had made. And when Stalin moved against the 'accursed kulak' the Left opposition was so imprisoned by its analysis that it collapsed around Trotsky. At last the 'centrist bureaucracy' had made its 'left turn' and *en masse* they capitulated to Stalin leaving only a confused and thoroughly disoriented rump behind.

When collectivisation came the alliance between the workers and the peasants was smashed and peasant opposition was ferocious. The procurement of grain did increase, but only at a fantastic cost. Millions of animals were slaughtered in retaliation and hundreds of thousands of peasants died in famine conditions. Agricultural output did not regain its 1926-28 levels until the mid-1950s. The political effects were equally telling. Collectivisation, combined with a repressive nationalities policy, produced such peasant disaffection that when the Nazis invaded in 1941, many villages welcomed them with open arms until they were quickly disabused of the idea that any salvation lay in that direction either.

There have been many attempts to show that collectivisation was a necessary solution to the problems of the 1920s. None of them is secure. Those that are not simple apologetics slide over the social significance of the industrialisation drive and rest upon *post hoc* rationalisations that are not supported by the evidence. Labour, for instance, was released by collectivisation for urban industry but there was no 'need' for it to occur in this manner. Reserves already existed amongst the urban unemployed, and in the countryside millions of underemployed peasants could have been released by a more constructive policy. The brutal reality of 'feeding the towns' turned out to be rationing and inflation running riot on the black market. The hardship this brought was certainly far greater than the hardship of the crisis that is said to have necessitated collectivisation.

Above all the argument that collectivisation was a form of 'primitive socialist accumulation' can no longer be sustained. The peasantry did not render a 'tribute' to the state and the working class, as even Bukharin thought. It is now known that such was the chaos and destruction that, in order to keep up agricultural production even at much reduced levels, it was necessary to push back into the countryside with one hand what was taken with the other.

In this sense it was not the peasantry who paid for industrialisation. The additional surplus for increased accumulation came from the towns — from the workers themselves. Just as the major part of accumulation in every other country has come from surplus value exploited from workers so it was in the Soviet Union too.[23]

The 'best' that can be said for collectivisation is that, having embarked on industrialisation, it made certain that rural conditions were so bad that, in spite of the appalling urban situation, no-one was tempted to return to the village. The traditional ties with the land that had characterised the previous first-generation factory workers in Russia were thus eliminated once and for all. It was in this sense that the detailed control and terror in the countryside made possible the generation of a surplus in the towns by eliminating any escape route.

In all of this then, the case for the validity of Bukharin's original perception of relations with the countryside still stands. But his conception of the worker-peasant alliance was broader than just an analysis of relations between the town and the country, worker and peasant. It was founded upon a different conception of planning and the market to that of most of his critics on the Left.

The Plan and the Market

Bukharin has often been portrayed as a supporter of what is now called market socialism. This is the argument that a socialist economy can only work if it retains the basic market mechanism and categories of capitalism albeit within the confines of 'nationalised' or 'socialised' state property. In fact, Bukharin did not argue either that the market was socialist or that socialism would mean a market-based economy. What he did argue was that the market could not be abolished at a stroke and that 'we are approaching socialism precisely through market relationships'.[24] In so far as the mass of the Bolsheviks accepted NEP there was nothing particularly original in this: these basic principles were common to the economic discussions in the 1920s. Bukharin's real originality lay in the way in which he conceived of planning and the market being able to express the same essence. To see the importance of this it is first necessary to summarise the major alternative view, that of E.A. Preobrazhensky.

Preobrazhensky saw NEP as a dialectical unity of the *contradictory* forces of planning and the market. The former expressed the law of value and the latter what he termed the 'law of primitive socialist accumulation'. There existed, therefore, two methods for the distribution of labour time and 'one system is bound to engulf the other'. In the short term, they represented a unity in the sense that planners could not simply escape voluntarily from the law of value. They had to work on the basis of an understanding of it and the way it could interact with primitive socialist accumulation. Since the market was linked to the peasants there had to be an active policy of price intervention from the state sector to transfer resources from the peasants to the state. This would lead to economic development and give that development a socialist character by placing it more firmly in the hands of the state. In this way the law of value could be overcome.[25]

The difficulties with this argument are fairly clear. What Preobrazhensky did was to counterpose the market and planning as two exclusive categories, defined basically on the distinction between state and private property. In this way socialism became identified with a shift towards the state sector. In practice Preobrazhensky's argument was much less crude than this. Like Bukharin he laid stress on the form of the state and working-class control. The shift to the state sector was only a necessary condition for socialism, not a sufficient one.[26] Nevertheless, the drift towards the collapse of his argument into a concern for legal forms is unmistakeable. It bore political fruit when Stalin moved to increase the power of the state in 1928 and Preobrazhensky was one of the first of the oppositionists to capitulate.

Bukharin firmly rejected this opposition of plan and market. He argued that socialist planning could consciously dominate and work through both forms. In the light of this, NEP was less a contradictory unity than a dynamic equilibrium of plan and market. The problem was not, therefore, to 'engulf' the market but consciously to limit its effects.

Such a process could not be understood outside of state policy, yet this is what Bukharin claimed Preobrazhensky was trying to do in both his methodological approach and in his invention of a 'law' like that of 'primitive socialist accumulation'. It was the workers' state which would lead the transition to socialism by 'the transformation of anarchic laws [of capitalism] into laws which are known and consciously applied'. To appreciate this it was absolutely essential to understand the nature of the originality of the base and superstructure relationship under the dictatorship of the proletariat where the workers' state is 'the collective directing subject'. In this sense a 'law' only has the force of law because it is policy, not because, as in Preobrazhensky's formulation, it reflects some transcendent, immanent necessity of industrialisation. By failing to investigate this Preobrazhensky was led to consider 'the plan, with the subject of the plan, planning without the planning organs, rationality without any precise place to locate it'.[27]

The idea of something having a lawful character outside of this was simply a mystification.

The difficulties of this mystification could be seen when the content of the 'law of primitive socialist accumulation', based upon unequal exchange with the peasants, was examined. When, for instance, did 'primitive' socialist accumulation end and 'socialist' accumulation begin? Was not the whole thing based on no more than a 'perfectly monstrous analogy'? Here he could draw on Lenin's own criticisms when he had used the term himself in his *Economics of the Transition Period*. Lenin had written that the use of the term (which Bukharin put in a different context) was, 'extremely unfortunate. A childish game in its imitation of terms, used by adults.'[28] Moreover, in so far as the 'law' might have practical consequences, did it not threaten to 'annihilate' precisely the political basis of the workers' state in the form of the workers' and peasants' alliance?[29]

Bukharin certainly put his case with an excess of polemic. Preobrazhensky never spoke, as Bukharin implied, of sucking the peasants dry or exterminating peasant undertakings. Nor was Preobrazhensky's case the same as Trotsky's, although Bukharin succeeded, much to Trotsky's helpless annoyance, in tarring them with the same brush.[30] But behind all this there was a serious critique which, wanting though it was in part, failed to elicit a satisfactory reply from Preobrazhensky.

At the root of the theoretical cleavage is an issue which today still dogs the debate on both capitalism and socialism. What Preobrazhensky did was to reduce capitalism to commodity production which in its turn was narrowly identified with the market. This was completely against the whole tradition of Bukharin's work. In his very first book, written in 1914, he had written that 'capitalism is the developed form of commodities production, characterised not by exchange *per se*, but by *capitalist* exchange. . . . An analysis of capitalism therefore involves . . . an investigation of the specific structure of capitalism itself.'[31] What defines capitalism for Bukharin is the dominance of capital and value to which the commodity form was itself subordinated.[32] One aspect of this can be found in Bukharin's analysis of the world economy and state capitalism which we examined earlier. There he argued that even though commodity production was partially negated, the anarchic drive to expand capital and value continued to operate and enforce its domination throughout the world economy. Now he turned this argument to the transition to socialism. For Bukharin the central question was not the abolition of the market as a form but the abolition of the imperatives of the self-expansion of value, the abolition of the capital relation. The real centre of the transition was therefore the attempt consciously to control society.

By contrast, Preobrazhensky's focus on 'the market' as a form and its juxtaposition to 'the plan' represented a basic fetishisation of categories. In this Preobrazhensky was not alone. A whole tradition of Marxist theorising in the 1920s tended to reduce Marx's analysis of capitalism to a focus on markets. This led to what Peter Binns has termed the 'fetishism of "commodity fetishism"'.[33] This involved an obsession with the commodity form which led to the erection of a basically static conception of capitalism as a market form and a misunderstanding of the very dynamic of capitalism and the way in which it tends to modify both the market and the commodity as it develops. The result was (although Bukharin never put it as pointedly as this) that Preobrazhensky, starting from a misconception of the nature of capitalism, was led to a misconception of the real nature of the transition and a treatment of it in terms of abstractions like 'the market' and 'the plan'. It is here also that one finds the theoretical roots of Preobrazhensky's later political capitulation to Stalin for, at least temporarily, he came to believe that at long last the 'plan' was engulfing the 'market'.

The Political Logic of 'Snail's Pace' Accumulation

It should now be possible to understand more clearly the political analysis that lay behind Bukharin's attitude to accumulation in the 1920s. Perhaps the most famous and distinctive statement associated with Bukharin at this time is his call,

> we must say to the entire peasantry, to all its different strata: enrich yourselves, accumulate, develop your farms. . . . A proper solution of the problem must be motivated by recognition that the prosperous farms have to be developed in order that aid may be provided to the middle and poor peasants.

Following this the economy, because of its dependence on agriculture and the peasantry, would develop at a 'snail's pace' drawn along by the 'peasant nag'.[34]

In putting this argument Bukharin was not suggesting that the level of accumulation was subject to economic limits, although these may have been present as well. Nor was he suggesting that it was necessary to encourage the kulaks as a class. Rather, what he was emphasising was the policy which had to be followed if the *political* conditions on which the worker-peasant alliance turned were to be met.

To maintain this alliance politically certain economic policies were necessary which ran counter to those suggested by Preobrazhensky. In particular, state industry should not aim to reap the benefits of 'monopolistic parasitism' by setting high prices for goods sold to the peasantry. It should aim at low prices to satisfy peasant needs and so draw the peasantry into contributing voluntarily to accumulation on the basis of its own prosperity. This was the same way that the working class would act, consciously (in theory) generating a surplus for accumulation. In essence, therefore, Bukharin saw that accumulation was limited by the need to maintain a certain proportionality in the economy which, going beyond any immediate economic factors, reflected the fact that neither the peasantry *nor* the peasants could be exploited in a workers' state.

For Preobrazhensky, by contrast, it was only the working class which set a limit to accumulation. As he described it in *The New Economics*,

from the moment of its victory ... [it] is transformed from being merely the object of exploitation into being also the subject of it ... its own labour power, health, work and conditions ... constitute a definite barrier to the tempo of socialist accumulation, a barrier which capitalist industry did not know in the first period of its development.[35]

The peasantry, on the other hand, are analysed as a third force located outside the embryonic socialist system. There they appear as the object of the workers' state, something to be manipulated in its interests.

In this way Bukharin arrived at a position where he argued that any speed-up in the rate of accumulation threatened to break the workers' state politically. In terms of the argument he put in the mid-1920s neither forced collectivisation nor forced industrialisation could solve the problems of the transition for the new state. On the contrary, they would compound them and, worse still, threaten to redefine the problems by politically redefining the nature of the state. As a result he closed off both collectivisation and industrialisation as possibilities.

Here we can see the crucial weakness in the traditional account that has been given of Bukharin's position. This has pictured the problem, not in terms of the intractable political reality of Russia in the 1920s, but in terms of a lack of an industrialisation programme in Bukharin's analysis. According to Moshe Lewin, 'Bukharin's blatent weakness during the 1924-26 period was that he had no serious programme for industrial development to offer *at this stage*.'[36] What was necessary in the light of this type of argument was to append such a programme to Bukharin's 'plan' for the peasantry. But we can now see that this was not so. The absence of a 'serious programme for industrial development' in Bukharin's analysis was neither fortuitous nor was it a 'blatant weakness': it was a direct and necessary consequence of his political estimation of the situation in Russia. To introduce such a programme into his analysis would fundamentally conflict with his assumptions at this time. Obviously the speed of the snail could be varied, it could be prodded to move at a faster pace, but what could not be done was to make the snail run with the speed of a hare, unless, of course, there was some way of turning the snail into the hare, but then we would be dealing with a very different animal and a very different type of society.

The Impasse

In this way, then, the case for Bukharin's perception of the internal nature of the transition to socialism and the central role of the worker-peasant alliance still stands. But, with the advantage of hindsight, we can also see how this analysis was leading him into an impasse. The more general presumption behind Bukharin's discussion was that the growth of the early years of NEP could continue indefinitely. If there had already been progress in the work of building 'socialism in the first years of the peace', he asked, then what reason was there for suggesting that there would be a regression in the future? His answer was that there was no reason at all, 'on the contrary . . . conditions . . . suggest the likelihood of *far greater successes* in the future'.[37] But for this to be the case then the framework of NEP had also to be capable of being extended into the future. To industrialise at a 'snail's pace' and in the process gradually to perfect the forms of socialism implied both the maintenance of domestic and international stability. But could Russia remain a 'bucolic idyll' given both the internal and external strains that it faced in the inter-war years?

Because of the unattractiveness of the periods of war communism and the Five-Year Plans it is tempting to juxtapose the NEP to them as an alternative model of development. Unfortunately, though, the

survival of NEP depended upon more than just the questions of relations with the countryside and the compatability of plan and market.
The fact that Bukharin could show that a major threat of destabilisa-
tion did not arise in either of these areas did not mean that there was
no threat, or that NEP was without other contradictions. Certainly it is
possible to find elements of NEP that are capable of generalisation, but
taken as a whole the relative 'peace and tranquility' of this time reflected
a temporary equilibrium of contradictory forces in a rapidly changing
situation. It is hard to see how this could endure when the forces that
gave rise to it were in flux. Indeed, the period of high NEP lasted no
more than two to three years at the most. In the economy, for example,
strong centralising tendencies were already emerging in 1925 and
1926.[38] Viewed in this perspective, rather than as an abstract model,
it can be seen that 'pluralism and diversity' were not created by NEP.
Instead NEP itself flowed from the existing but temporary balance of
forces in society at large. Bukharin, for all his intellectual brilliance, was
blind to this and so have been those of his modern supporters who have
tried uncritically to adopt the perspective he developed in these years.

The result of this was that Bukharin's discussion of the transition
was necessarily a partial one because it abstracted from the totality of
pressures in NEP. Therefore, whatever its validity in one direction, it
was compromised by its blindness in another. For example, the idea of
the worker-peasant alliance guided by the workers' state should have
immediately raised the question of the integrity of that state as a
workers' state. As we have seen, in practice, the civil war had forced the
abandonment of the democratic state forms created by the Revolution.
Yet far from these being fully restored under NEP, one must search
hard to find any serious attempt to re-establish them. Indeed, the
trends went increasingly in the opposite direction. Where then did this
leave Bukharin's concept of the workers' state that was supposed to
guide and fill out the content of the worker-peasant alliance?

This problem also arises from another direction in his analysis. If, as
Bukharin had argued against Preobrazhensky, the plan and the market
are capable of expressing the same essence, then why should that
essence necessarily be a socialist one? In his analysis of state capitalism
Bukharin had shown that capital could fuse with the state to create
total state capitals which could use both plan and market forms to
organise themselves internally in order to meet the anarchic demands of
competition in the world economy. What prevented this analysis being
applied to Russia now? At the level of theory Bukharin had a clear
answer, state capitalism was negated by the political domination of the

new state by the working class. But what of the level of practice? Was this a description of the way the state was run under NEP, and if it was not then where was the guarantee that the 'negation of state capitalism' could not itself be negated?

The urgency of answers to questions like these increased after 1926. It was then that the framework of NEP came under increasing pressure both as a consequence of the contradictory internal demands that were put upon it and because of the Soviet perception of their isolation in a hostile world economy. In the face of this a focus on the worker-peasant alliance by itself was insufficient. At a more general level the Soviet state was increasingly losing control of the situation and was becoming its victim, a process only aided by its increasing internal bureaucratisation.

The problem that this presented for Bukharin's analysis is fairly obvious. His general argument had been that during the transition to socialism the revolutionary state must seek to uproot the old relations of production. But what would happen if the revolutionary state lost control of the social processes above which it was trying to rise? Detached from its revolutionary base, could it not become the agent of precisely those same relations of production that it was trying to overthrow? Following the logic of his argument this question ought to have been of central concern to Bukharin. It was not, and in this we shall find the theoretical roots of his political downfall.

The fact that Bukharin did not find an answer to these problems raises the question of whether the answer can be found within the terms that he set for himself. In fact there was, and is, a very obvious solution at hand but it was one that he was prevented from following up because of his entanglement with the theory of socialism in one country. It is here that we return to the 'paradox' with which we began this chapter and the need to overcome the limitations of both Bukharin's and Trotsky's contemporary arguments. If the revolutionary state was under pressure because of its backwardness *and* isolation then did not the answer lie in throwing all the available resources into breaking that isolation and pushing the revolution outwards? In this way, as part of an ever widening socialist bloc, the international pressures could have been eased and the more advanced countries could have used their superior productivity to provide the materials needed to cement the alliance of workers and peasants. Far from it being the case that the worker-peasant alliance provided the basis for socialism in one country when it is set in the context of the general problems of NEP, it is rather the case that international revolution is the precondition for the development of the worker-peasant alliance. In this sense Bukharin's internal policy would seem to fit in far more closely with a policy of permanent revolution than that of the opposition and, in particular Preobrazhensky, who did not share his insistence on the narrower political limits to accumulation. But, as we have seen, Bukharin had already ruled out any exploration of this avenue through his links with Stalin.

This failure by Bukharin to carry through the logic of his argument into the international sphere left him in a dilemma. Once the pressures of accumulation began to mount he found himself pushed beyond the limits he had set for the worker-peasant alliance. On the one hand, the pressures of isolation were pushing the regime towards a much faster pace of development and, on the other hand, his analysis ruled out the possibility of that development without threatening the worker-peasant alliance. Something had to give. In the real world he could not maintain both his emphasis on 'snail's pace' accumulation and his support of socialism in one country. When the break came it was in his analysis of the internal situation.

In terms of Bukharin's political biography it is not hard to see why he was forced down this path. His entanglement with the theory of socialism in one country was not just theoretical. In the mid-1920s he had become, in E.H. Carr's phrase, Stalin's 'willing henchman' in the debates with the opposition. Part of the reward for the sorry role he played here was his position in the Communist International where he had a heavy responsibility for the policies which contributed materially to the defeat of the revolutionary movement, especially in China in 1927. Under the weight of the opposition's attack, Bukharin resorted to bluff and bluster to weather the storm of criticism. By this time he was in no position to rethink his commitment to the theory of socialism in one country. The chains that bound him were too tight and they would now drag him down. Having once supported Stalin, he now found himself dependent on Stalin for his protection.

As a consequence, after 1926 Bukharin was impelled to transcend the limits he had himself set to accumulation. He did not, of course, ever go as far as Stalin, and at the last moment he drew back in horror at the prospects of what would happen under the first Five-Year Plan, but he had already moved sufficiently to cut the ground away from his analysis and the basis of developing a real alternative to Stalin. To examine how this occurred more closely we must turn to look in some detail at the degeneration of the Revolution and Bukharin's reaction to it.

Notes

1. N.I. Bukharin, *Historical Materialism. A System of Sociology* (1921), New York: International Publishers, 1925, p. 261.

2. In his autobiographical essay, written in 1925 and translated in G. Haupt and J.J. Marie (eds), *Makers of the Russian Revolution*, London: Allen & Unwin, 1974.

3. The development and problems in Trotsky's analysis can easily be traced in the successive volumes of the *Writings of Leon Trotsky, 1929-1940*, New York: Pathfinder Press, various dates, which cover the pamphlets, articles, letters and interviews of his years of exile. There is a hostile but pointed evaluation of his detailed misunderstandings in the crucial years 1929-31, as reflected in the *Bulletin of the Opposition*, A. Nove, 'A Note on Trotsky and the "Left" Opposition, 1929-31', in his *Political Economy and Soviet Socialism*, London: Allen & Unwin, 1979, pp. 44-62. For a more substantial theoretical critique, see J. Molyneux, *Leon Trotsky's Theory of Revolution*, Brighton: Harvester Press, 1981, chapter 4.

4. This misunderstanding was reflected in the way in which the Left continued to describe the Stalinist group as 'centrist' into the 1930s (i.e. vacillating between Left and Right but leaning to the latter) long after both the Left and the Right had been destroyed.

5. A. Ciliga, *The Russian Enigma*, London: Ink Links, 1979, Book 3, chapters V-VIII. The other leading figure of the Left opposition was Christian Rakovsky. Unfortunately, there is no adequate study of his analysis nor its links to that of Trotsky. It clearly remained trapped in the general assumptions of the Left but it was superior to Trotsky's in a number of respects. In his discussion of the bureaucracy, for example, Rakovsky saw both that the problem was not simply one of non-proletarian elements — solid workers could become just as bad bureaucrats as anyone else because, detached from their working-class base there were certain 'occupational risks of power'. Secondly, he saw that the bureaucracy was coming to possess the state as its own personal property. But as with all contemporary discussion of the problem, these insights were weakly developed and caught in an inconsistent framework. Rakovsky, ill and increasingly isolated, held out from capitulation to Stalin until 1934. See F. Conte, *Un révolutionaire-diplomate: Christian Rakovsky. L'Union soviétique et L'Europe (1922-1941)*, Paris: Mouton, 1978, chapters IX-XIII, and the collection of his writings in C. Rakovsky, *Selected Writings on Opposition in the USSR, 1923-30*, London: Allison & Busby, 1980.

6. R. Day, *The 'Crisis' and the 'Crash': Soviet Studies of the West (1917-1939)*, London: New Left Books, 1981, chapter 3.

7. N.I. Bukharin, *The Road to Socialism and the Worker-Peasant Alliance* (1925), translated in N.I. Bukharin, *Selected Writings on the State and the Transition to Socialism*, Nottingham: Spokesman, 1982, pp. 291-2.

8. By contrast, in 1918 in the debates over Brest-Litovsk the thought that 'in preserving our socialist republic, we will lose the chance of an international movement' had been uppermost in his mind. *The Bolsheviks and the October Revolution. Minutes of the Central Committee of the Russian Social-Democratic Labour Party (Bolsheviks) August 1917-February 1918*, London: Pluto Press, 1974, p. 176.

9. N.I. Bukharin, 'The International Situation', *International Press Correspondence* (hereafter *Inprecor*), vol. 7, no. 14, 17 February 1927, p. 283.

10. Ibid.

11. Ciliga, *op. cit.*, p. 14. He reports a speech by Rykov 'in which he declared

that had the opposition been listened to, the Soviet state would have supported the Chinese Revolution. But fortunately "we" had not allowed ourselves to be dragged into it and thus avoided war with Great Britain.'

12. Conte, *op. cit.*, p. 218. Rakovsky's cry was from the heart, Trotsky later identified the cold logic of the doctrine of socialism in one country: 'The new doctrine proclaims that socialism can be built on the basis of a national state *if only there is no intervention*. From this there can and must follow . . . a collaborationist policy towards the foreign bourgeoisie with the object of averting intervention, as this will guarantee the construction of socialism, that is to say, will solve the main historical question. The task of the parties in the Comintern assumes, therefore, an auxiliary character: their mission is to protect the USSR from intervention and not to fight for the conquest of power. It is, of course, not a question of the subjective intentions but of the objective logic of political thought.' Quoted in Molyneux, *op. cit.*, p. 148.

13. Bukharin's crucial role here is beyond the scope of this work but it generally needs re-examination. The lack of a detailed discussion of the whole episode is a serious deficiency in Cohen's biography.

14. *The Road to Socialism*, *op. cit.*, pp. 265-6.

15. V.I. Lenin, *Collected Works*, vol. 33, Moscow: Progress, 1965, pp. 467-75.

16. 'The Letter of an Old Bolshevik', in B.I. Nicolaevsky, *Power and the Soviet Élite*, London: Pall Mall Press, 1966.

17. N.I. Bukharin, 'A New Revelation Concerning the Soviet Economy or how to Destroy the Worker-Peasant Bloc' (1924), in N.I. Bukharin, *Selected Writings on the State*, *op. cit.*, p. 162.

18. *The Road to Socialism*, *op. cit.*, pp. 230-1.

19. 'A New Revelation', *op. cit.*, p. 167.

20. *The Road to Socialism*, *op. cit.*, p. 260.

21. E.H. Carr, *Socialism in One Country*, vol. 1, London: Macmillan, 1958, pp. 329-32; see also M. Lewin, *Russian Peasants and Soviet Power*, London: Allen & Unwin, 1968, chapters 2 and 3.

22. N.I. Bukharin, 'Notes of an Economist' (1928), translated in N.I. Bukharin, *Selected Writings on the State*, *op. cit.*, pp. 314-16.

23. This judgement is based on the fundamental revision of our view of collectivisation made by the Soviet historian A.A. Barsov, which confirmed the scepticism already expressed by some historians about the traditional view of the decisive contribution of the peasantry to accumulation. The debate initiated by Barsov's work is well summarised by R. Munting, *The Economic Development of the USSR*, London: Croom Helm, 1982, pp. 106-10. The precise contribution of the working class is still being disputed (see, for example, D. Morrison, 'A Critical Examination of A.A. Barsov's Empirical Work on the Balance of Value Exchanges Between the Town and the Country', *Soviet Studies*, vol. 34, no. 4, October 1982) so it is worth stressing that this debate will not invalidate the general revision. The increase in investment was so great compared to the size of the agricultural sector and its troubles that the biggest contribution to the increase in accumulation had to come from the working class. This can also be tentatively confirmed by tracing the whole issue from the workers' side, a task which has yet to receive adequate attention.

24. *The Road to Socialism*, *op. cit.*, p. 260.

25. E.A. Preobrazhensky, *The New Economics*, Oxford: Oxford University Press, 1965; E.A. Preobrazhensky, *The Crisis of Soviet Industrialisation*, New York: M.E. Sharpe, 1979.

26. See D. Filtzer, 'Preobrazhensky and the Problem of the Soviet Transition', *Critique*, no. 9, Spring Summer, 1978.

27. N.I. Bukharin, 'Le problème des lois de la période de transition' (1926), in

96   *The New Economic Policy*

N.I. Boukharine, *Le Socialisme dans un Seul Pays*, Paris: Union Générale d'Éditions, 1974, pp. 45-6.

28. N.I. Bukharin, *The Economics of the Transformation Period*, New York: Bergman, 1971, pp. 110, 191, 223.

29. N.I. Bukharin, 'A new revelation', *op. cit.*; N.I. Bukharin, 'La loi de l'accumulation primitive socialiste ou pourquoi il ne faut pas remplacer Lénine par Préobrajenski' (1926), in N.I. Boukharine, *Le Socialisme dans un Seul Pays*, *op. cit.*

30. See R. Day, *Leon Trotsky and the Politics of Economic Isolation*, Cambridge: Cambridge University Press, 1973, pp. 147-8. There is a valuable discussion of the differences between Preobrazhensky and Trotsky by Jean-Luc Dallemange, 'Le concept d'industrialisation dans l'analyse de Trotsky', in Fondation Giangiacomo Feltrinelli, *Histoire du Marxisme Contemporain*, tome 5, Paris: Union Générale d'Éditions, 1979, pp. 137-77.

31. N.I. Bukharin, *The Economic Theory of the Leisure Class*, New York: Monthly Review Press, 1972, p. 50.

32. This difference is apparent even in terminology: Preobrazhensky persistently refers to 'commodity capitalist relations' whereas Bukharin discusses 'capitalist commodity relations'.

33. P. Binns, 'Law and Marxism', *Capital and Class*, no. 10, Spring 1980, pp. 105-9.

34. N.I. Bukharin, 'Concerning the New Economic Policy and our Tasks' (1925), in N.I. Bukharin, *Selected Writings on the State*, *op. cit.*, pp. 197-8.

35. Preobrazhensky, *The New Economics*, *op. cit.*, p. 122; for Bukharin's and Preobrazhensky's joint declaration that the working class cannot be exploited in a workers' state, see their *The ABC of Communism*, Harmondsworth, Middlesex: Penguin Books, 1968, p. 312.

36. M. Lewin, *Political Undercurrents in Soviet Economic Debates*, London: Pluto Press, 1974, pp. 14-16.

37. N.I. Bukharin, *The Road to Socialism*, *op. cit.*, p. 292.

38. See, for example, V. Bandera, 'The Market Orientation of State Enterprises during NEP', *Soviet Studies*, vol. 22, no. 1, July 1970, pp. 110-21.

6 THE DEGENERATION OF THE RUSSIAN REVOLUTION

Discussing the potentialities revealed by the experience of the Paris Commune, Marx wrote that

> the political rule of the producer cannot coexist with the perpetuation of his social slavery. The Commune was therefore to serve as a lever for uprooting the economic foundations upon which rest the existence of classes, and therefore class rule.[1]

This passage well defined what the Bolsheviks saw as the tasks of the dictatorship of the proletariat in Russia. In our previous discussion we have suggested that they became separated from this in two ways. First, against the background of the intensification of the civil war, the state ceased to be a 'commune state'. Secondly, isolated socially and politically at home and internationally, it proved impossible to 'uproot the economic foundations ... of classes, and therefore class rule'. It remains now to bring these two strands together and examine how Bukharin failed to develop a coherent analysis of the way in which the Revolution was degenerating and what consequences this had for his theory and politics at the end of the 1920s.

In a review of Lenin's *State and Revolution* written in early 1918 Bukharin summarised what he saw as both the theory and the reality of the dictatorship of the proletariat. 'The proletarian dictatorship,' he wrote, 'is not a parliamentary republic with all its decorations but a *commune-state*, without a police force, without a standing army, without officialdom etc.'[2] As a description of what existed in Russia between October 1917 and May-June 1918 this picture did have a real basis in fact. Already before October the rise of factory committees and soviets based upon the workplace, housing committees, even committees of schoolchildren had created what the French historian Marc Ferro has called a state without a head. This was a new state rising from below. True it was more developed in some places than in others (in Petrograd, for example) but it nevertheless reflected a real mass mobilisation of the Russian working class in a search for new means of democratic control. Indeed, in a sense Ferro's image is more appropriate than Trotsky's description of the situation as one of 'dual power' for in the end Kerensky's official government had no power:[3] its base had been captured and partially rebuilt from below. In October 1917 the Bolsheviks attempted to supply this embryonic state form both with a new head and a skeleton to contain its vital organs.

It was the civil war which brought a halt to the building of this new state. By 1921 the picture had changed radically in favour of a bureaucratic and highly centralised state machine. The Bolshevik Party too had been forced the same way by the terrible demands imposed by the civil war.[4] It was these years which laid the basis for the further degeneration in the 1920s to a final result far distant from the hopes of October.

At one level Bukharin was far from blind to this. As we saw in Chapter 4, during the civil war he stressed the military character that the dictatorship of the proletariat was forced to assume. He also saw the dangers that were created by the destruction of the base of the new state — the working class. As early as March 1918 he had warned of these.[5] By the end of the civil war he was talking of a 'social crisis in the midst of the working class'.[6] But what implications did this have for the nature of the state? That he should find difficulty in answering this question is, at first sight, surprising since on a number of occasions he provided a picture of the possible future himself.

The Threat of State Capitalism

In his book *Historical Materialism*, Bukharin noted that there was an implicit contradiction between the decline of the productive forces, which he saw as inevitable in all revolutions, and the development of working-class consciousness. As a result he argued that

> there will inevitably result a *tendency* to 'degeneration' i.e. the excretion of a leading stratum in the form of a class-germ. This tendency will be retarded by two opposing tendencies: first, by the *growth of the productive forces*; second, by the abolition of the educational monopoly.[7]

The implication is clearly that the revolution could degenerate into a form of state capitalism as this 'class-germ' developed. This followed from his earlier analysis of the nature of the transition. If, as he had argued, the transition involved a dialectical reversal of 'state capitalism' so that politics came to dominate economics then if political control were to slip the 'dialectical reversal' would cease and the old content be re-established, albeit perhaps clothed in a new institutional form.

A short while later he returned explicitly to this theme. Discussing the nature of NEP he rejected the argument that it was any form of state capitalism but he did allow that

> of course, our economic system can be changed into 'true' state capitalism, if the class struggles in the sphere of direct processes of production and in the political sphere result in the loss of power by the working class.[8]

Nor were comments like this exceptional, they re-occur at a number of points in his later works too.[9] But by far the most developed consideration of this possibility of a degeneration into a form of state capitalism came in a discussion of the problems of cultural revolution that Bukharin wrote in 1923. There he suggested that the working class

> can mechanically defeat the adversary, it can smash the bourgeois clique to smithereens, physically seize everything but it can still be eroded by the much more cultivated forces of its adversary, not in the form of struggles and confrontations ... but by a process of slow and progressive social evolution. This danger exists for any working class which has taken power.

In this situation, he went on,

> members of the technical intelligentsia, a party of the bourgeoisie, let us say concretely, the entrepreneurs, tradesmen, etc. and, in addition, perhaps even members of our own Party could form a new class which would detach itself, little by little, in an imperceptible but complete way from the proletarian base and which could become a new social formation.

This was a danger, not of open defeat by counter-revolution, but of an 'internal reconstitution' of a new bourgeoisie based on the state.[10]

In this way Bukharin opened up the possibility for an analysis of the degeneration of the Revolution which, unlike that of the opposition, did not depend upon the situation in the countryside and the threat of the kulaks. Rather, the undermining of the commune-state through the loss of working-class control would itself allow forces within the state to come to the fore, forces which would constitute in their own right the social basis of a new class. Unable then to uproot the economic foundations of class rule, these forces would themselves become agents of the old relations of production on which the revolution had broken its back.

The possibility that this was an accurate description of what was actually occurring as a result of both the civil war and NEP is a striking one. But Bukharin only put this possibility abstractly and in outline. To have developed the analysis he would have had to have focused both on the degeneration within the state itself and on the totality of relations in which that state was imprisoned, both domestically and internationally in the 1920s. Yet in practice this was not what he was prepared to do. To have developed an analysis of the degeneration of the state, Bukharin would first have had to have recognised its extent but, as we shall see, he was unable to do this. To have examined the limitations on the power of the Soviet state he would have had to have confronted his ideas about socialism in one country with his analysis of capitalism as a world economy. Again he could not do this. The result was, we shall argue, that in spite of having within his grasp the possibility of an understanding of the nature of the revolution's degeneration he was unable to take hold of it. As a consequence, the revisions in his analysis which he made after 1926 and which have attracted so much attention recently both played directly into Stalin's hands and, to the extent that they offered any alternative at all, constituted only a more moderate version of industrialisation on the backs of the working class as it was eventually carried out under Stalin. In this sense Bukharin's policies came, in 1927 and 1928, to be distinguished only in degree from those of Stalin and the ground around him. They were not different in kind.

Fetishising the State

In the first flush of revolution Bukharin had described the various threads that tied the working class to the dictatorship of the proletariat in a higher democracy. He then commented that 'these organisational threads never break. They are the normal way of social life. This is what fundamentally distinguishes the Soviet Republic from all other forms of state life.'[11] And yet we know that the strain on these threads did increase to breaking-point as a result of subsequent events. The breaks were not repaired in the 1920s, with the result that the degeneration did threaten to lead to the creation of a state fundamentally *in*distinguishable from other forms of state life. Far from adjusting his analysis to this Bukharin retreated to a substitution of Party for class and then the leadership of the Party for the Party. He could not see that this posed any problem for his understanding of the situation.

The consequences of this was that on every occasion when the question of state capitalism arose in the 1920s he could answer, no — not yet. What prevented it applying was the working-class nature of the state. But to maintain this in the face of growing evidence to the contrary meant that his argument had to become increasingly abstract and fetishised. The nature of the state had been established in 1917, it might be overthrown at some date in the future (and especially if current policies were reversed) but there was no question of this happening here and now. Class, Party and state all remained bound in an unbroken union. Thus when he did raise the question of degeneration he did so only at such an abstract level that he could not apply it to the reality around him.

There was perhaps some excuse for this in the period of the civil war, but this almost immediately disappeared. In *Historical Materialism* he was still writing as if it were October 1917. Thus,

> we may *distinguish* between class and Party, as we distinguish between the head and the entire body, but we cannot *discuss them as opposites*, just as we cannot cut off a man's head, unless we wish to shorten his life.[12]

But worse was to come. As the actual problem of the separation of state and Party from class became more acute, Bukharin's claims of the contrary became even more shrill. Thus in 1925 he proclaimed that 'the development of present-day society in the direction of socialism is guaranteed by the fact that the working class holds power and that we have a revolutionary dictatorship, or undivided rule.'[13] This was reflected in the Soviet state, 'yes, we have incontestably built a new state. And this is the premise that allows us to continue our economic development.'[14]

It is the complete and utter unreality of this type of comment which makes his discussion of the state and Party so banal in the 1920s. Whereas once he had argued that the question of the state was 'the fundamental and principal question of the entire practice of the revolutionary class', he now dealt with the problem himself simply by assertion and rhetoric. It is no wonder that Preobrazhensky could despair of his 'causistical smart-aleckries' when Bukharin tried to attack 'Trotskyism' and 'the grey emptiness and dreariness of his book on Kautsky' where an unravelling of the nature of the state should have been the centre-piece.[15]

Part of the difficulty that Bukharin had in coming to terms with this problem was that the degeneration had also affected the Bolshevik Party deeply. How much the Party and state had intertwined and changed by the mid-1920s does not need to be stressed at length. Suffice it to say that already in 1921 a quarter of the Party's member-ship had been purged for 'bureaucratic deformations' but, of course, many of those doing the purging were no less guilty and some no doubt more guilty than those purged. Then, whereas Lenin had wanted a further cleansing of the Party on the principle 'better fewer, but better', the Party leadership mockingly commemorated his death with the so-called 'Lenin enrolment'. The already weakened political consciousness of the Party was diluted even more by a mass influx of new members. The result was inevitably to strengthen further the power of the Party apparatus: 'We could no longer recognise the old Party of the revolu-tion,' wrote the oppositionist Victor Serge — and with reason.[16]

In the face of this Bukharin seemed to live in a cocoon. Even his sympathetic biographer, Stephen Cohen, is forced to talk of his 'chronic public optimism' and his 'romance of the Party'. For Bukharin it was the unsullied character of the core of the Party that held together the perspective of building socialism in one country. The consequences of this position were catastrophic. Theoretically, Bukharin saw the possi-bility of degeneration but he now drew back from investigating its reality. This led him politically to play Stalin's game until it was too late. His doubts and criticisms, even his final fight against Stalin as part of the so-called 'Right opposition', were all developed behind closed doors. Significantly, in his 'Notes of an Economist' (his 1928 attack on Stalin) in spite of calling for a return to the commune-state of the early revolution, Bukharin still argued that 'the basic leadership and the most important questions must be decided more resolutely, more strictly (but with greater thoughtfulness) *"at the centre"*.'[17]

This treatment of the class nature of the state as an abstraction accounts for an apparent peculiarity of his thinking in the 1920s. Bukharin was, in fact, a major critic of bureaucratisation, the low quality of the Party, the ineffectiveness of the youth organisation (the Komsomol), the use of appointments, and so on. Indeed, when Trotsky needed to support his arguments he could substantiate his case against the Party by quoting Bukharin at length.[18] Bukharin even took up the question of Stalin's treatment of the Georgians when everyone else, including Trotsky, kept quiet. Throughout the 1920s he went further and made constant efforts to raise the demand for increasing the cultural and political level of the working class and for opening up the state. But all of this could coexist with his political assessment of the state because he never turned his attack from one on bureaucrat*ism* into one on the bureaucr*acy* as an independent social force.[19] Nor did he attribute a class basis to the problems he discussed. The threat of the bureaucracy remained an abstract possibility. The actual bureaucratic degeneration that was taking place was only an external force acting on the state. As late as 1928 he could write that, 'the pores of our gigantic apparatus also harbour elements of bureaucratic degeneration', thus separating 'our gigantic apparatus' from the 'bureaucratic degeneration'.[20] And when events pushed him further he was able to go beyond formulations like this in only the vaguest of ways.

There is an obvious contrast here not only with the Left opposition and Trotsky, but with Lenin as well. In a famous exchange in December 1920 Lenin spoke of the Soviet state as being a 'workers' and peasants' state'. He was immediately interrupted from the floor by Bukharin who asked 'what kind of state? A workers' and peasants' state?' Some weeks later Lenin, reflecting on what he had said and the criticism implied in Bukharin's interruption, wrote a more considered definition of the Soviet state:

> I was wrong and comrade Bukharin was right. What I should have said is, 'A workers' state is an abstraction. What we actually have is a workers' state with this peculiarity, firstly, that it is not the working class but the peasant population that predominates in the country, and, secondly, that it is a workers' state with bureaucratic deformations.'[21]

This exchange has usually been interpreted in Bukharin's favour. At no point in their considered writing do Lenin, Bukharin or, for that matter, Trotsky refer to the state as a 'workers' and peasants' state'. The Soviet state for them was a workers' state and in this sense Bukharin was correct to challenge Lenin's offhand comment. Subsequently he took Lenin's first qualification about the peasantry to heart and developed his analysis of how the workers' state would have to lead the worker-peasant alliance. But Lenin's second qualification, about the problem of 'bureaucratic deformations', seemed to pass him by. By contrast, this was a danger that Lenin was constantly preoccupied with. Even in the midst of the civil war he had argued that

the more resolutely we now have to stand for a firm government
... the more varied must be the forms and methods of control from
below in order to counter every shadow of possibility of distorting
Soviet power, in order repeatedly and tirelessly to weed out
bureaucracy.[22]

Later, Lenin likened the Soviet state to a car in which the driver had no
control. The Bolsheviks had been forced to reincorporate much of the
old state machine to win the civil war, 'that was our misfortune'. Far
from these elements coming in practice to be held in Bukharin's 'web'
of workers' power, the state machine was taken 'over from Tsarism
and slightly anointed with Soviet oil', 'the apparatus we call ours, is in
fact still quite alien to us; it is a bourgeois and Tsarist hotch-potch.'[23]

Why then was Bukharin unable to see the depth of the problem
facing the Soviet state? A full answer would have to weave together a
number of personal, political and theoretical strands. Here we shall only
draw attention to the most important of them.

One aspect is the way in which the discussion of the degeneration of
the Revolution and state was carried out in the 1920s. The simple fact
is that no political grouping or individual really understood what was
happening. The difficulty was that they did not all share the same misunderstanding. The result was an asymmetry of error which blinded
each side to what was correct in the other's analysis and which led to
arguments being damned in total. This fog of misunderstanding has
still not entirely cleared.

The various oppositions, for example, constantly drew attention to
the dangers of degeneration in the state. But then having identified the
danger they went on to see its basis as the situation in the countryside
and the threat of the kulaks. For the reasons we have already examined,
Bukharin could not accept this, nor could he accept the policies which
flowed from the analysis or the opposition's attempts to find solutions
in what he contemptuously dismissed as 'beautiful paper plans'. But the
danger was that in correctly dismissing the larger part of the analysis
of the causes of the degeneration that the opposition put forward he
would be blinded to the reality of the degeneration that, however
inadequately, they were trying to come to terms with. This, of course,
is what happened.

In their turn, the opposition did exactly the same thing. Seeing
clearly the inadequacy of Bukharin's 'chronic optimism' about the state
and Party, they failed to see the force of his critique of their own
position on the causes of the degeneration and they held equally

inflexibly to the notion that the real problem was the 'danger from the Right' which Bukharin himself was supposed to represent. In this confusion the only person to gain was Stalin. Tragedy, wrote Hegel, is not the conflict of right and wrong but of right and right. Here the situation was somewhat different. It was a tragedy of two different partial truths masquerading as whole truths.

Bukharin, then, could not share the opposition's analysis and fell into the trap of missing the substance of their complaints about the state. He was confirmed in this even more by his own lack of political sensitivity. Bukharin's theoretical brilliance was never complemented by his political sense. This weakness had been manifested on a number of occasions in the past. The weakness in his position, for example, on the national question, Brest-Litovsk, the trade union debate have been the subject of detailed and perhaps exaggerated criticism in the litera-ture on Bukharin.[24] But they illustrate a real problem that perhaps no-one was more aware of than Bukharin himself.

It is in this context that one must view the political significance of his relationship with Lenin. Lenin was, he said, 'my revolutionary teacher'. Trotsky was later to write bitterly of the sycophantic nature of Bukharin's intellectual relationships, but this view is far from the truth. More perceptive was Trotsky's private assessment in 1921, that 'Bukharin is always in front, but he's always looking over his shoulder to make sure Lenin isn't far behind.'[25] This was not an image that Bukharin would have objected to. More often than not his disagree-ments with Lenin were not theoretical but over the relationship of theory to political practice. Here Lenin was a guiding force who con-stantly restrained his leaps from the right theory to the wrong politics. For Bukharin, Lenin's greatest strength was his ability to develop the 'arithmetic' of practice from the 'algebra' of revolutionary theory. This, he recognised, was his own weakness. It was also this that Lenin was partly identifying in his *Testament* when he doubted if the Party's 'leading theoretician' really understood dialectics.

When Lenin died a crucial prop was pulled away from Bukharin's Marxism. Worse than this, he then characteristically tried to replace it by schematising Lenin's thought and so compounding the schematisa-tion that characterised his own understanding of political issues. It was Bukharin who, in the first instance, was largely responsible for launch-ing the idea of 'Leninism' as a codified system.[26] Here he was trying to grasp at the inner content of revolutionary Marxism that he felt he lacked. The struggle for Lenin's theoretical heritage had, of course, much wider implications than this in the context of Soviet politics in

the 1920s.[27] But it would be foolish to ignore the intensely personal
way in which Bukharin needed his own concept of 'Leninism' to sustain
his Marxism, and how this increased his tendency to abstraction and
retreat into old formulae when faced with the concrete political problems of the time.

Finally, we can also note how Bukharin was constrained by his
personal identification with the fortunes of the Revolution and the
Bolshevik Party. This was far more complete than that, say, of Trotsky.
Bukharin had invested too much of himself to be able to make the
necessary break with the Party, and this underpinned his failure of
political nerve. Indeed, in this respect it was precisely his awareness of
the possibility of the Revolution degenerating into a form of state
capitalism that made him unwilling to go further than he did. If he
allowed that an internal class reconstitution was actually taking place,
would this not mean that everything had been in vain? This was his fear
and he could never face it squarely.

It is interesting at this point to look at his hysterical attack on the
opposition in 1923. Here he tried to destroy their case by driving it to
its logical conclusion. 'Trotsky,' he wrote,

> claims that the Central Committee represents the *bureaucratic*
> 'fraction'. One can only agree with him that bureaucratisation of the
> ruling party would be extremely dangerous. But if the Central
> Committee represents this bureaucracy ... why allow it to *remain*?
> Why not *drive it out*? The country's ruin, social treachery, degenera-
> tion into bureaucracy — surely these are sufficient causes to *drive*
> such a Central Committee *out*?[28]

And indeed why weren't they? But it was only a short time after
Bukharin's challenge that Trotsky made his famous declaration before
the 13th Party Congress in 1924:

> Comrades, none of us wants to be or can be right against the Party
> ... the Party is the sole historical instrument that the working class
> possesses. ... It is only possible to be right with the Party and
> through it since history has not created any other way to determine
> the correct position.[29]

Two years later Trotsky could still not bring himself to break with the
Party and the opposition split on this issue. Then when he was forced
into a break he still clung to the straw that something of the Revolution

continued through his thesis that Russia under Stalin was a degenerated workers' state.

Bukharin could not go even this far. The personal cost was too much for him. He even rejected the opportunity of emigration when it came in the 1930s. He summed up his feelings at his trial in 1938 when he asked, 'If you must die, what are you dying for?' And if he should live, 'Again what for? Isolated from everybody, an enemy of the people, in an inhuman position, completely isolated from everything that constitutes the essence of life.' One would have to be a Trotsky to go, he said, but Bukharin was no Trotsky and so, if reality did not fit the analysis, then so much the worse for reality.[30]

Socialism in One Country

Failing to see the reality of the degeneration of the state, Bukharin was then unable to go on and draw the links between his analysis of the world economy and its corrosive impact and events in Russia in the 1920s. He was not unaware that the area of leeway for the Soviet state was limited. In his book *Historical Materialism* he had written that

> the concentrated authority of a class, its state authority, is a power: but this power is not *unlimited*. No force can transcend its own limits. . . . In other words: the alteration in the economic conditions that may be obtained with the aid of the political lever is itself dependent on the previous state of economic conditions.[31]

But he did not then go on to analyse the significance of this. In fact, acceptance of the theory of socialism in one country implied a much more voluntaristic conception of the transition. The power of the 'political lever' — the state — was now apparently such that it could indeed begin to transcend its own limits. This was a step that Bukharin never made in theoretical terms but it was the step he was increasingly forced to make in practice as the logic of socialism in one country began to unravel itself.

But a deeper problem lay behind this in the way that the reconstitution of the old relations of production was a product both of internal and external pressures in the 1920s. It is important to stress this interaction not only because Bukharin failed to see its significance but also because this failure to examine the totality of relations in which the Soviet state was located has been carried over into the recent literature.

The French Marxist Charles Bettelheim, for example, has presented an analysis which is strikingly 'Bukharinist' in its stress on the need to maintain a positive relationship with the peasantry. But, like Bukharin, Bettelheim also accepts as well the possibility of socialism in one country. His central criticism of Bukharin is that he and the Bolsheviks did not go far enough to both 'make the revolution and make production'. Ultimately, they chose to make production and expand the economy leaving the Revolution and the changes in relations of production to make themselves. What was necessary, however, according to Bettelheim, was the active advancement of what he calls 'proletarian social practices'. Such practices (which are not defined) would have served to give more political force to the worker-peasant alliance. Bukharin's failure was that he went insufficiently far in developing these practices. Whilst he was more far-sighted than most Bolsheviks in his discussion of the worker-peasant alliance, he nevertheless remained tainted by what Bettelheim terms an economistic focus on expanding production.[32]

Bettelheim's discussion can be criticised on a number of grounds, but what is of interest here is the way in which although trying to broaden Bukharin's perception he retains its basic narrowness through his implicit acceptance of socialism in one country. The problems of Russian society are reduced to internal ones linked to the abject poverty and backwardness that the Revolution inherited.

But the power of the old relations of production to bend back the state into its capitalist negation are more widely based than this. Capitalist relations of production are not just forged at the factory gate. They exist as the whole totality of relations that capitalism needs to reproduce itself. And these relations, as Bukharin himself had earlier stressed, transcend national boundaries. They are constituted ultimately at the level of the world economy where the interaction and competition of many capitals receives its fullest expression. Whether its leaders liked it or not, Russia remained trapped within this totality of relations of production. The first step towards their fracture had been made within the factories through the soviets; the creation of the dictatorship of the proletariat gave the possibility both of welding together a new society from below and of holding off the pressures from above as it tried to reflect the attempt consciously to subordinate social processes to popular control. But now the soviets were empty shells, the state itself increasingly out of control, and the pressure of world capitalism increasing at all levels. To understand the degeneration, therefore, it is necessary to relate both the internal and the external pressures to one another.

It is insufficient to focus on the worker-peasant alliance by itself even if it is broadened in the way Bettelheim suggests. The recent historical work which supports Bukharin's assessment of the agrarian question, and which we too have followed, says nothing of these wider contradictions. The agricultural situation and the problems of the state must be placed in this totality of relations not abstracted from them. Stalin, above all, understood this. For him the agrarian situation was firmly subordinate to the wider issue of Russia's position in the world economy and the necessity to respond to the pressure of world imperialism. And today, too, without an understanding of this there can be no adequate explantion of what happened.

Here at least there was something in Preobrazhensky's argument that the transition period is built upon contradictions. But the central contradiction was not the internal one he saw of the plan and the market. It lay rather at the level of the relation of the transitional society to the world economy. Preobrazhensky, however, resolved this, albeit tentatively, by the state monopoly of foreign trade which he pictured as a weak 'Chinese Wall' between the Soviet economy and the world economy. When he argued therefore for international revolution it was less because of the need to challenge the pressure of the old relations of production working through the corrosive influence of the world economy — these were held off by the 'Wall' — rather, it was because he could see no other solution to the *technical* difficulties *within* Russia of a faster pace of industrialisation. By contrast Bukharin was not so naive. He saw nothing particularly socialist in protectionism, even with a state monopoly of foreign trade. Indeed, he had at one time been prepared to consider its being disbanded. What negated the old relations of production was not an institutional form which capitalist countries were already beginning to adopt, but the revolutionary state itself which through its political control sought to impose itself on the old relations and consciously negate them.

But once the state itself ceased to express a genuine democratic control, would it not simply find itself internalising the very pressures it was supposed to ward off? The logic of Bukharin's analysis of world capitalism certainly pointed in this way. The state could not forever stand naked against this pressure. In this way the central contradiction became expressed in the form of whether the pressure of world capitalism should be challenged through international revolution, or whether it should be challenged on the terms set by the system and the creation of a state in its image. It was in this way that the internal reconstitution of classes occurred in relation to the external pressure of the world economy.

This is why, when Stalin defined the pattern of Soviet development, and when he called

> no comrades ... the pace must not be slackened! ... To slacken the pace would be to lag behind; and those who lag behind are beaten. ... We are fifty or a hundred years behind the advanced countries. We must make good this lag in ten years. Either we do it or they will crush us[33]

he echoed the words of the Tsarist Finance Minister Witte, some 30 years before. Witte too had recognised that 'he who does not go forward will for that very reason fall backward'; 'International competition does not wait.'[34] In the intervening years the imperatives forcing industrialisation had not changed, they had intensified as international competition had shifted into a new gear. Such pressures could only be broken if the system that produced them was broken too.

Where Bukharin erred was in failing to see that his own analysis of the world economy mapped out a picture of this very situation. He had shown how states acted as agents of capital accumulation, and how the pressure of the law of value operated in various distorted forms through the world economy. Viewed in this perspective there is nothing particularly peculiar about the Soviet experience after 1928. Industrialisation completed the subordination of the Soviet economy to the world economy and married the state and capital. In so doing it realised in an extreme degree tendencies which, as Bukharin had stressed, were imminent in capitalism as a world economy.

The idea, which derives in part of Preobrazhensky, that industrialisation in the Soviet Union somehow denies the law of value, lies buried deep in the acres of print discussing development plans for industrialising states. What had been negated was not the law of value, if by that is meant the social validation of labour through the anarchic competition of many capitals. What had really been negated was a pattern of development based upon the maximisation of a static comparative advantage. Resources were now to be marshalled under the Five-Year Plans in such a way as to drive the economy forward to create an industrial base to compete with the advanced capitalist states. The root of that drive and the pattern of development were socially validated and remain socially validated by capitalism as a total world economy. The real uniqueness of the Soviet experience lies elsewhere, in the way in which this form of state capitalism developed out of the wreck of a revolution that had promised to change the capitalist world — not to outdo it.

Bukharin's 'Counter-Programme'

Having explored the way in which Bukharin's fetishism of the state and his assumption of socialism in one country compromised his discussion we are now in a position to evaluate the way in which he developed his analysis after 1926. As we saw in Chapter 5, by this time he had arrived at a theoretical *cul-de-sac*. In the first place, he had argued that the political conditions of the worker-peasant alliance set a clear limit to the pace of accumulation. In the second place, socialism in one country meant that any funds to increase the pace of accumulation would have to be found internally. Now, however, the pressures both of the internal degeneration and changes in the world situation forced him to break out of this *cul-de-sac*. The way he did this was not by challenging the second assumption of the realism of socialism in one country, but by beginning to stretch the political limits he had set to accumulation and eventually transcending them altogether.

At the centre of Bukharin's new perspective was his support for a faster pace of industrialisation. What was necessary, he now argued, was a policy of 'optimal' growth which would accelerate industrial development over the long run. This was the position adopted at the 15th Party Congress in 1927:

> we must not adopt a maximum rate of accumulation for the *coming year* or for a period of several years, but must instead begin with a relationship that will guarantee the most rapid rate of development over the long run.[35]

This new emphasis on a faster accumulation demanded the maintenance of a dynamic equilibrium in the economy. It needed scientific planning and respect for existing constraints for 'with an incorrect policy the cost of the process as a whole might be no less than the cost of capitalist anarchy.' Plans had to be drawn up consistently and implemented consistently.

To achieve this Bukharin argued that it was necessary to continue to work within the formal structure of NEP and in particular the market. The market would act both as a vehicle for the plan and a corrective mechanism. Already the state was taking on too much and creating bureaucratic inefficiency. Accumulation should not provide the excuse to accentuate these negative features. By renewing the market and pluralist elements of NEP it would be possible both to have growth and to contain its negative side-effects. This was Bukharin's interpretation of the policies adopted in December 1927 and it is implicitly shared, though less often explicitly stated, by those who have attempted to rehabilitate Bukharin's 'counter-programme' as an alternative. According to Lewin, Bukharin 'developed a set of theses that amounted to a full-fledged counter-programme for Russia's road to socialism as opposed to the one the majority leaders were embarking upon.'[36]

Circumstances, however, gave Bukharin little time to articulate his new policy in any positive way. Within months he was having to fall back on it as a defence against the super-industrialisers who wished to go far beyond the goals and tempos of 1927. Bukharin soon realised that the real challenge to NEP came from those associated with Stalin. As early as 1925 Party members in Gosplan and non-Party specialists had begun to press for higher targets. Increasingly these optimistic voices became more urgent and gathered support. To the leadership these forecasts must have seemed like a godsend. Subject to the push of the growing bureaucracy for increased rewards, they also faced increasing difficulties at home and abroad. Internally, problems in grain procurement were mounting and these were increasingly seen as a 'crisis'. Then externally, in 1927, a war scare seemed to put the whole basis of the regime into question just at the moment when the opposition was pressing home its attack. Shrinking from a revolutionary response, a dash for growth and a rapid military build-up seemed to be the answer. Here the attraction of increased tempos and the prospect of soaring growth curves was obvious. At first affecting Stalin's associates, this attitude spread as the difficulties increased until a majority of the Politburo saw no other alternative than a policy of increased collectivisation and industrialisation. Then, once initiated, the process soon came to have a vicious logic of its own which overturned NEP and eliminated the final remnants of the revolutionary achievement.

This turn was made possible by the political defeat of the Left opposition in 1927. The arena was now open for Stalin's final conflict with Bukharin and the so-called 'Right opposition'. Bukharin immediately responded within the leading circles of the Party by attacking the policies of 'madmen'. The prospect of defeat forced him to seek wider publicity. At first this was relatively open. In the autumn of 1928 he published his famous 'Notes of an Economist' in *Pravda*. Ostensibly an attack on the opposition, this was in fact a thinly-veiled attack on the new line, and a defence of the decisions of the Party Congress. Here he attacked the whole basis of collectivisation. The grain crisis was not the product of some mysterious kulak threat. To the extent that it existed at all, it was the product of economic causes, not political revolt. It had to be dealt with by economic measures, not administrative actions. Collectivisation had to be related to the existing poverty of the countryside and limited by it. It was something which, in the short term, could only offer the possibility of a few gains and only then if it proceeded slowly.

In industry too the economy was already strained and unbalanced. It was absurd to demand more.

> if there are no bricks, and if they *cannot* be produced beyond a certain volume in the current season (for technical reasons), then we *must not* draw up construction programmes in *excess* of that limit ... factories and housing facilities cannot be manufactured from air.

Then too, he stood out more generally against the continued growth of centralised power — 'we have overcentralised everything to an excessive degree. We must ask ourselves: Should we not take a few steps in the direction of the Leninist commune-state?'[37]

But however strong the argument was that he put forward, the fact was that lacking any control of the Party apparatus, Bukharin was increasingly outmanoeuvred and deprived of support. Stalin's final victory came early in 1929 and in April, at the Central Committee meeting, his policies were overwhelmingly confirmed. The new Five-Year Plan was endorsed, a Politburo censure of Bukharin upheld, and he was removed from his official posts at *Pravda* and in the Communist International. But for the next few months the necessity and perhaps the will to go beyond this did not exist. Then, in August 1929, he was finally deprived of any independent voice and subjected to what Cohen has rightly called 'a systematic campaign of political defamation unsurpassed in Party history'.[38]

Yet Bukharin's argument of this time has survived and it is not difficult to see that a large part of the attraction that it has lies in the possibility it seems to offer of industrialisation within the assumptions of socialism in one country but without the accompanying horrors of Stalin's regime. It is this type of argument that lies behind the judgement of the Soviet dissident historian Roy Medvedev, when he writes that, without Stalin, 'we would, probably, have been able to obtain significantly greater results.'[39]

However, the issue that this type of assessment raises does *not* relate to Bukharin's critique of Stalin and industrialisation as it was actually carried out. Half a century later the power and the vision of his attack is still there. Russia did industrialise but in a totally chaotic fashion. In the countryside collectivisation brought man-made famine and death on a then unparalleled scale. In industry all concern with balance and with equilibrium disappeared as all of Bukharin's forebodings about the effects of madcap industrialisation were fulfilled.

With the intensification of political and economic pressure, the original Five-Year Plan was transformed. Rationality disappeared as competing groups strove to outdo one another. The 'madmen' whom Bukharin feared did not stop at simply doubling tempos. The voice of moderation became the voice of defeat. Riazanov caustically summed up the situation at the Party Conference in April 1929 when he commented that 'every speech ends. . . . Give us a factory in the Urals and to hell with the *RIGHTS*! Give us a power station and to hell with the *Rights*!'[40] This was not planning but a totally chaotic form of development. But there was an overall rationale within the chaos. It was perverted but real, and it lay in the attempt to beat capitalism at its own game. The anarchy that this entailed meant that the question of genuine socialist planning never arose.

In fact the Five-Year Plan was defective even from the start. It was not even consistent in its gross magnitudes, let alone its petty details. Even in the most favourable circumstances it could not have worked in its existing form. The consistency that Bukharin had demanded had not been achieved. Most importantly, success would have required that the standard of living be slashed although the planners were unaware of the full extent of this. But the problem did not arise in any planned form. The drive to push up targets destroyed the plan. Priority sectors became autarkic empires at the cost of fantastic waste and duplication. The plan's assumptions about agriculture were destroyed by collectivisation; those about international trade by the world depression which led to forced isolation as balance of payments pressures mounted. The consequences were those that Bukharin had predicted. Each problem, each imbalance, was met by administrative pressure leading to further 'organised chaos'. 'Our operative planning has neither hands nor feet,' reported one Soviet newspaper in 1932.[41] The essence of this process has been summed up by Moshe Lewin:

it was the unplanned character of the whole process which forced upon the state ever more 'planning' meaning simply the need to enlarge upon the scope of administrative controls, and the takeover of the whole national economy by state apparatuses.[42]

The plan was dead. What was left, and what remains today, is a bureau-cratically controlled economy whose institutional framework was created as the *ad hoc* response to the contradictory pressures of unplanned industrialisation in a hostile world economy. This was and is the reality of the world's 'first planned economy'.

In all of these areas history has come down on Bukharin's side and vindicated his opposition to a degree which in his wildest nightmares in 1928 and 1929 he could not have imagined. But this does not show the validity of his own position as an *alternative*. The problem here is, as Stephen Cohen has pointed out, not one of personality as some, like E.H. Carr, have suggested.[43] It lies in the fact that a critique, no matter how perceptive, does not automatically become an historically viable alternative. Even less is it necessarily a socialist alternative, and here we come to the crux of the issue on which the accounts to build Bukharin as *the* opponent of Stalin flounder. It is not sufficient to judge Bukharin's alternative as a technical matter of alternative growth rates, nor is it sufficient to dismiss the political corrolaries of Bukharin's position such as his support for Stalin as 'shortsightedness', as does Moshe Lewin.[44] To judge Bukharin's position seriously requires us to take a position on the nature of the transformation that occurred in the Soviet Union and to place Bukharin's analysis within the context of this. Had he remained in power the absurdities of the industrialisation drive, the purges, the repression would all have been less and this is important. But the decisive issue is, would the character of the trans-formation of Soviet society have been changed? And here we have the heart of the difficulty of Bukharin's 'counter-programme' because, on examination, it can be shown to embody much the same set of assump-tions as the majority line. These assumptions were not matters of 'high theory' but the very basis of the logic of forced industrialisation and they broke apart the earlier theoretical framework Bukharin had fought for.

Over the Edge

The essence of the shift in Bukharin's position lay in the weakening of his resolve that neither the working class nor the peasantry could be subjected to exploitation to generate a surplus for accumulation. More-over, this weakening came at precisely the time when already the reality of the life of workers was far removed from that implied by the rhetoric of the time. Within the factories the old forms of the labour process had been re-established over the heads of the working class rather than through it. The pressure to increase productivity was increasingly being felt and the attraction to various forms of scientific management served only to increase the alienation of workers. But the increasing adoption of explicitly capitalist organisational forms and the general pressure for output only reflected the more general processes at work in Russian society and the loss of real power by the working class. The result was that by 1928, in spite of an increase in the standard of living, there was already a clear switch away from consumption to investment. Given the already wretched conditions of workers at the time, such a burden was becoming excessive even within the framework of NEP.[45]

The demand to implement the decisions of the 15th Party Congress has to be seen against this background. Bukharin might now reject his earlier idea that Russia could ride 'to socialism on a peasant nag' but the resources for accumulation still had to be found from somewhere. A harder line in the countryside would help but he was aware of the limits to this. The other obvious source was the working class. Indeed, an investigation of the base-line (minimum) version of the original draft of the Five-Year Plan has shown that the only way in which its limited targets could be met in the specified time was through a major cut in personal consumption.[46] But not only would such a cut have to be imposed on the working class but it also threatened to bring with it resistance if the limited rights of workers were left unchallenged. In practice, of course, when Stalin imposed an even greater cut it was premised on the wholesale removal of workers' leaders at all levels and the complete reorganisation of trade unions into transmission-belts for the state's drive to increase productivity. Bukharin never had to consider such a course, but was the emasculation of workers' rights any less implicit in his own programme?

It was in this way that Bukharin began in practice to overstep the limits to accumulation that he had earlier set. Given the goal of a faster industrialisation the resources had to be found at home. This is why he was increasingly forced to resort to euphemisms like the need for 'belt-tightening', in explaining the basis of his alternative.

But the weakness of his counter-programme goes deeper still. The goal of socialism in one country forced Bukharin to overstep the limits of his earlier position also in the sense that he was now forced to tie the dynamic of industrialisation to the logic of external circumstances. Socialism in one country needed time and this meant that the 'socialist fatherland' had to be defended. He could argue, as he did, that the

Soviet Union 'must be protected to the last drop of blood . . . everything must be sacrificed; everything staked in order to protect this
country at any price, whenever danger threatens it', but the logic of this
position increasingly pushed him to support as the primary means of
defence a conventional military response. The armed might of the
Soviet state had to be built up so that it was equal to that of its potential adversaries. Again Stalin's solution of an arms drive and a rapid
military build-up might have been more extensive than Bukharin
envisaged but it was essentially his solution too.

In fact the strategic logic of this position had already begun to
emerge in the mid-1920s. A military reform in 1924-25 put the main
emphasis on the development of a standing army (a characteristic
Bukharin had earlier denied to the commune-state). But with such an
army necessarily went both a hierarchical internal organisation and a
conventional fighting role. Yet Bukharin had earlier also argued that the
relationship of the armed forces to society was a specific one. Capitalism
and the transitional society both gave rise to different forms of military
force based upon different social relations.[47] But here the reverse
seemed to be occurring. Similar forms were being created, and once
created they then implied a degree of militarisation in society at large
just as in the West. The logic of this aspect was already being drawn out
by Voroshilov and other leaders in 1927.[48] Bukharin, of course, was not
notable by his opposition to these moves. On the contrary, this position
was worked out and affirmed both within the Party and the Communist
International while he was still playing a leading role.

This military logic of socialism in one country crystallised as the
international situation deteriorated. Bukharin certainly pushed a softer
line than Stalin and he rejected the idea of 'social fascism' for the
nonsense that it was, but he still remained imprisoned by the thesis that
he had helped to create. This was forced home by the war scare in the
first nine months of 1927. During this time there seems to have been a
genuine concern that war with the West was about to erupt. Historians
have not been able to find clear evidence for this in western diplomatic
papers but this did not alter the way in which the threat was perceived
and felt in Moscow. One possible response to this was to try to recreate
a genuinely revolutionary foreign policy and to throw the emphasis
onto the spreading of international revolution. This was the argument
that the opposition put forward. 'The development of the [interna-
tional] revolutionary movement . . . is the primary fundamental
guarantee of the inviolability of the USSR and the possibility . . . of
peaceful socialist development.'[49] But Bukharin was now pushed in

another direction. In the wake of the defeat of the Chinese Revolution and the policies he had supported there he saw the way to face the western powers as involving a change in the internal pattern of resource allocation. What was needed, he argued, was 'a whole series of measures which could secure our independence from economic ties.'[50] Far from breaking out of the isolation being an immediate imperative, he was led to espouse policies which implied precisely the opposite. It was in this way that the international situation acted directly to preclude any possibility of steering a course between the goal of accumulation and the continued survival of any remains of working-class power and the worker-peasant alliance.

The impact of this new perception of the military situation can clearly be seen in later discussions. It contributed materially to the re-evaluation of the possibilities of accumulation and a higher rate of growth. In this sense, even for Bukharin, the discussions at the 15th Party Congress involved much more than an intellectual argument about the degree of capacity in the economy. The whole issue now had a new dimension.

Bukharin subsequently tried desperately to apply the brakes in 1928. He insisted that the threat of war was less than Stalin and others suggested. Western capitalism was still subject to a degree of 'relative' and 'temporary' stabilisation.[51] Yet he had implicitly conceded his position. What seemed to separate him from the others was the question of time and the unwillingness to follow through the logic of socialism in one country.

Stalin had no doubt about what this meant — the task was not simply to increase the tempos but to catch up with Western Europe in the shortest possible time. But Bukharin drew back from the consequences of this. His subsequent 'bewilderment' — the term is Stalin's — became apparent at the meeting of the Central Committee in July 1928. There Bukharin could correctly point out that 'we are moving all the time in contradictions', but these were contradictions that he could not resolve himself for the premise of his argument was now no different from the group around Stalin. Trying to gain his point he argued, 'If we want to catch up with Western Europe — *and we want to do this* — if we want to increase the tempo of accumulation for socialist industry — *and we want to do this . . .*' But then how could he develop his argument? He was left an easy target for the taunts of Voroshilov when all he could do was to list difficulty after difficulty,

Voroshilov: Give us your panacea.

Bukharin: I don't want to give a panacea, and you, please, don't make fun of me. I want to say that the reconstruction period quite naturally evokes a series of complications and difficulties . . .

In fact, of course, he had no panacea. He could paint a frightening picture of the dangers and plead for the Party to 'fulfill the basic testament of Lenin', but he could provide no other general answer than to qualify the one that was in the process of being made. It was easy for Stalin then to deflate his arguments, to the general laughter of his supporters, with the Russian proverb, 'A fearful dream, but God is merciful'. The stakes were high, but Bukharin had allowed himself to become a willing participant at the table.[52]

Bukharin's weakness at this meeting was a personal turning-point. Although Stalin made some concessions Bukharin now had no doubt of his own impotence. The very next day he made a fateful secret contact with Kamenev that Stalin was later to use against him. Here he revealed the depth of the divisions and their personal and political dimensions. Stalin's concessions had only been made 'so as he can cut our throats'. But what could Bukharin now do in his own defence? Even had the remains of the opposition been willing to support him — which they were not — his room for manoeuvre was limited. Stalin now held all the cards — 'We don't want to come forth as schismatics, for then they would slaughter us.'[53]

Insight in Defeat?

In the years between his defeat in 1929 and his dramatic appearance as a defendant in the third and greatest purge trial in 1938 Bukharin cut a far from impressive figure. Yet this destruction was never total. In an article he wrote in 1930, and which was immediately read as a thinly-veiled attack on Stalin although it was ostensibly about the Pope and the Jesuit tradition, Bukharin described how

> every member of the order must submit to his superior 'like a corpse, which can be turned in any direction, like a lump of wax, which can be made to change its shape and strength in any direction'. This corpse is differentiated according to degrees of perfection: subordination of action . . . of will . . . of reason. When the last degree has been reached . . . we have the 100 per cent Jesuit.[54]

Bukharin was never that pliable, he never became the 100 per cent Jesuit. Stephen Cohen has attempted to argue that in these years Bukharin continued to put up major political resistance to Stalin,[55] but if this was so — and few have followed Cohen's estimation of Bukharin's role at this time — the character of this resistance was even more restrained than his opposition in the decisive years of 1927 and 1928. In the end, by 1937 and 1938, he was reduced to a stream of endless letters to Stalin: 'Dear Koba! Dear Koba! Dear Koba! And he got not one reply,' says Solzhenitsyn, catching the pathetic futility and despair of the situation.[56] Perhaps the final irony can be found in the moving last testament that he wrote for his young wife to memorise just days before his arrest: it was addressed, 'To a future generation of *Party leaders*'.[57] To the end he could not break completely free of his romance with the Party hierarchy and the Party itself.

And yet at the level of theory Bukharin still prided himself that he was a representative of the Marxism that had made the Revolution. Because of his connection with the development of so much of the Bolshevik analysis Stalin could only erect himself as the true inheritor of that tradition by attempting to destroy Bukharin's contribution. Against this onslaught Bukharin tried tenaciously to hold on to his position and its grounding in Marxism. Is there any evidence in this fight that he grasped at the argument we have put and came to see the degeneration of the Revolution as having culminated in state capitalism?

The evidence here is simply insufficient to support a strongly positive argument on this. What is not in doubt is that Bukharin at the least considered this as a possibility. This is the import of the two articles he published in *Pravda* in the lull between his defeat in April 1929 and his public disgrace in August of that year.[58]

Why Bukharin was allowed to publish these articles is not entirely clear. Richard Day has suggested that he may have been allowed the theoretical rope with which he would subsequently be hanged. If this is true, then in Day's view he made 'a bizarre political blunder' by taking up the opportunity afforded to him.[59] But whatever the explanation the theoretical significance of these pieces cannot be ignored.

In Chapter 3 we drew attention to the importance of these articles for the development of his general theory of state capitalism. Here Bukharin stressed the manner in which international antagonisms had grown as *laissez-faire* had given way to what a German economist, E. Schmalenbach, had termed 'chained capitalism' in an article published the previous year. At the same time, the fact that the subordination to the world economy was now more highly mediated (with the link to the market less direct) meant the development internally of 'organised chaos'. But Bukharin then went much further. He suggested that the target of these two pieces was as much the Soviet Union as it was the West. At this stage, Bukharin was in no position to make this connection explicitly but the hints are too strong to be ignored. As a description and analysis of the situation in the West in 1929 his discussion was prophetic but overdrawn. As a description of Russia in 1929 it seemed to apply directly, and just in case readers did not notice it Bukharin went on to draw their attention to the relevance of his picture: 'The Soviet reader,' he wrote, 'will be struck by the formal similarity between certain organisational problems' within the Soviet economy to those of state capitalism. *Of course*, he went on, these problems arose in a different form in the Soviet economy, but the features he drew attention to did not really clarify what this difference was. He noted, for example, that the Soviet bureaucracy was not staffed by members of a homogeneous class, but if there were class differences what was their basis and how were they manifested? Bukharin did not say, but he ended by saying that if the 'organised chaos' of western state capitalism was creating problems then 'in our own case the practice of socialist construction raises analagous problems and does so even more stubbornly.'[60]

We shall probably never be certain just how Bukharin wanted these two pieces to be read. Were they just a flippant means of attacking his critics with an embarrassing analogy? If they were, then Bukharin's 'political blunder' was truely 'bizarre' because it seems inconceivable that he did not have some inkling of their likely reception. If they were not meant to point in a political and theoretical direction, then why take the risk of publishing them at all in this form? If they were meant to point in this direction then how seriously had he really revised his theory? Unfortunately, it is just this kind of dilemma that we are left with when we encounter any piece written in 'Aesopian' language at this time.

In Bukharin's case, however, there is other evidence that might encourage us to lean towards a more serious treatment of these hints. Any interpretation of the Aesopian content of his writings in defeat must reflect the fact that he saw his theory of state capitalism as one of his central achievements. He made this clear in late 1930 when he was finally forced to make a public disavowal of his past. The grudging tones in which this was done were clear to all, and it is not surprising that his critics accused him of being 'two-faced'.[61] On his supposed deviation in his theory of state capitalism towards Hilferding's concept of 'organised capitalism' he had this to say:

as regards the question of 'organised capitalism' I admit my errors which Lenin exposed in my *Economics of the Transition Period* (1920). In my article, 'The Theory of "Organised Chaos" ', I attempted to proceed from the principles of Engels and Lenin and their programmatic works [*Critique of the Draft of the Erfurt Programme, State and Revolution* and others]. But as far as I used formulations which went beyond the limits of the formulations of Engels and Lenin or which deviated from those formulations I admit my errors here also. These errors were the reason for my articles in the spirit of organised capitalism. They proved politically damaging and were very correctly condemned by the decisions of the plenary session of the Executive Committee of the Communist International.[62]

The position that Bukharin adopted here was exactly the one he would later use in the purge trial.[63] He would admit the general charge and then proceed to defend himself by making nonsense of it in a detailed rebuttal under the cover of his admission of guilt. In the first place, referring the discussion back to his *Economics of the Transition Period* was a neat touch since we have seen that although Lenin was critical of a number of things Bukharin said, he did not reject the theory of state capitalism (read now 'organised capitalism') and he ended by warmly recommending the book as 'indispensable'. Then his theory had only led him to write *in the spirit of* 'organised capitalism'. He had gone *beyond the limits*, but who had set these limits? He had *deviated*, but here he was giving readers of his admission of guilt references to the basis of his position in the Marxist classics. His articles had proved *'politically damaging'*, but to whom? It is not surprising that such a performance caused his accusers to choke.

After this we are left with very little of theoretical interest. Bukharin continued to write mainly for the Soviet press as well as producing some longer pieces on science and technology. His one major work was a widely-read discussion of Marxism which has been called 'perhaps the last statement of classical Marxism to be published in Stalin's Russia'.[64] But while this piece echoes a number of Bukharin's earlier themes they are generally hidden beneath the surface. At one point, however, they did come up for an airing when Bukharin reminded his readers that the state was a guarantee of the process of exploitation which ought to be withering away and that

Marxism ... has nothing in common with its pitiful social-fascist caricature which goes back ideologically to Lassalle, growing with all its shoots into the ideology of the fascist 'National', 'caste' and 'corporative' state, with the proletariat completely enslaved to capital and its terroristic dictatorship, offered up under the pseudonym of the 'nation' and the 'whole'.[65]

Despite the obligatory praise for Stalin at the end of the article, comments like this got a little too close for comfort and Bukharin soon found himself under attack again for his theoretical 'errors' in the piece.

Beyond this a survey of his journalism is not particularly rewarding. Treated as an exercise in Kremlinology it can be made to yield something. His articles on fascism, for instance, like the comment above on 'social-fascism', can be interpretated as Aesopian attacks on Stalin's regime, and this may have been his intention. The pointers are few and the danger is obviously that given their sparseness one reads one's own predelictions into his writings. But this is not what is important. Even had Bukharin made no hint about the applicability of his analysis of state capitalism to the Soviet Union, the whole construction of his argument points that way. It is on this basis that Bukharin makes his claim on us. With his analysis of the world economy, the state and the transition he had taken Marx's own analysis forward a considerable way. That he too may have failed to complete his argument is no excuse for Marxists failing to do so today.

Notes

1. K. Marx, 'The Civil War in France', in K. Marx and F. Engels, *Selected Works*, London: Lawrence & Wishhart, 1968.
2. N.I. Bukharin, 'Gosudarstvo i revolyutsiya', *Kommunist*, no. 1, 20 April 1918, p. 19.
3. M. Ferro, *October 1917*, London: Routledge & Kegan Paul, 1980.
4. See R. Service, *The Bolshevik Party in Revolution*, London: Macmillan, 1979, especially chapters 5-7.
5. E.H. Carr, *The Bolshevik Revolution 1917-1923*, vol. 2, Harmondsworth, Middlesex: Penguin Books, 1966, p. 196.
6. N.I. Bukharin, 'La nouvelle orientation économique de la Russie des Soviets', *Bulletin Communiste*, vol. 2, no. 51, 17 November 1921, p. 856.
7. N.I. Bukharin, *Historical Materialism. A System of Sociology*, New York: International Publishers, 1925, pp. 310-11.
8. N.I. Bukharin, 'The Economic Structure of Soviet Russia', *International Press Correspondence* (hereafter *Inprecor*), vol. 2, no. 22, 21 March 1922, p. 165; *Pravda*, no. 30, 8 February 1922, p. 1.
9. See, for example, N.I. Bukharin, 'The International Bourgeoisie and Karl Kautsky, its Apostle', *Inprecor*, vol. v, no. 64, 13 August 1925.
10. N.I. Bukharin, 'Proletarskaya revolyutsiya i kul'tura' (1923). There is a

124   *The Degeneration of the Russian Revolution*

translation of substantial parts of this in F. Champarnaud, *Révolution et contre-révolution culturelles en URSS*, Paris: Anthropos, 1975, pp. 357-82. Note that Bukharin was quite prepared (in theory) to see that the new ruling class could have former workers at its core: 'if we imagine conditions in which a break is produced between the mass of the workers and a section which has risen from them we will find that a new class made up of ex-proletarians will be created.' Nor was this problem unique to Russia. Any revolution faced the danger of degeneration including, he stressed, revolutions in Germany and America where the working class was the strongest.

11. N.I. Bukharin, 'The Theory of the Dictatorship of the Proletariat', in N.I. Bukharin, *The Economics and Politics of the Transition Period*, London: Routledge & Kegan Paul, 1979, p. 51.

12. N.I. Bukharin, *Historical Materialism, op. cit.*, pp. 305-6.

13. N.I. Bukharin, *The Road to Socialism and the Worker-Peasant Bloc* (1925), in N.I. Bukharin, *Selected Writings on the State and the Transition to Socialism*, Nottingham: Spokesman, 1982, p. 263.

14. N.I. Bukharin, 'La situation intérieure de l'URSS', *Cahiers du Bolchévisme*, no. 20, 1 July 1925, p. 1295.

15. E.A. Preobrazhensky, *The New Economics*, Oxford: Oxford University Press, 1965, p. 9.

16. V. Serge, *From Lenin to Stalin*, New York: Monad, 1973, p. 40.

17. N.I. Bukharin, 'Notes of an Economist' (1928), in N.I. Bukharin, *Selected Writings on the State, op. cit.*, p. 328.

18. See L. Trotsky, *The Challenge of the Left Opposition*, New York: Pathfinder, 1975, pp. 148-50.

19. See D. Law, 'The Left Opposition in 1923', *Critique*, no. 2, 1973, for the importance and development of this distinction between the critique of *bureaucratism* and the critique of *the bureaucracy*.

20. N.I. Bukharin, 'Notes of an Economist', *op. cit.*, pp. 328-9. Bukharin was, of course, restricted in what he could say but this formulation should be compared with Rakovsky's in 1930: 'from a proletarian state with bureaucratic deformations – as Lenin defined the form of our state – we are developing a bureaucratic state with proletarian communist survivals.' Rakovsky held back still from concluding that this transformation of the state was complete but, he went on, if the process continued then the formation of a new *class* of rulers would be consolidated based on a new form of private property, 'the possession of state power'. Quoted in F. Conte, *Un révolutionaire-diplomate: Christian Rakovsky. L'Union soviétique et L'Europe (1922-1941)*, Paris: Mouton, 1978, pp. 255, 258.

21. Quoted in T. Cliff, *Lenin*, vol. 4, London: Pluto Press, 1979, p. 126.

22. Quoted in L. MacFarlane, 'Marxist Critiques of the State', in B. Parekh (ed.), *The Concept of Socialism*, London: Croom Helm, 1975, p. 178.

23. V.I. Lenin, *Collected Works*, 4th edn, Moscow: Progress, 1965, vol. 33, p. 428; vol. 36, pp. 605-6.

24. See S. Cohen, *Bukharin and the Bolshevik Revolution*, Oxford: Oxford University Press, 1980, *passim*.

25. Quoted in A. Rosmer, *Lenin's Moscow*, London: Pluto Press, 1971, p. 43.

26. See N.I. Bukharin, *Lenin as a Marxist*, London: Communist Party of Great Britain, 1925.

27. V. Gerratana, 'Stalin, Lenin and "Leninism"', *New Left Review*, no. 103, May-June 1977.

28. N.I. Bukharin, 'Down with Fractionalism' (1923), translated in T. Riha (ed.), *Readings in Russian Civilisation*, vol. 3, Chicago: University of Chicago Press, 1969, p. 541.

29. Trotsky, *op. cit.*, p. 161.

30. See G. Katkov, *The Trial of Bukharin*, London: Batsford, 1969.
31. N.I. Bukharin, *Historical Materialism*, *op. cit.*, pp. 264-5.
32. See C. Bettelheim, *Class Struggles in the USSR, Second Period: 1923-1930*, Hassocks, Sussex: Harvester Press, 1978.
33. J.V. Stalin, 'The Tasks of Business Managers' (1931), in J.V. Stalin, *Leninism*, vol. 2, London: Allen & Unwin, 1933, pp. 423-4.
34. Quoted in T. von Laue, 'The State and the Economy', in C.E. Black (ed.), *The Transformation of Russian Society*, Cambridge, Mass.: Havard University Press, 1960, pp. 215-16.
35. N.I. Bukharin, 'Notes of an Economist', *op. cit.*, p. 325.
36. M. Lewin, *Political Undercurrents in Soviet Economic Debates*, London: Pluto Press, 1974, p. 21.
37. N.I. Bukharin, 'Notes of an Economist', *op. cit.*, p. 328.
38. Cohen, *op. cit.*, p. 332.
39. R. Medvedev, *K sudu istorii*, New York: Alfred A. Knopf, 1974, p. 232.
40. Quoted in Cohen, *op. cit.*, p. 326.
41. Quoted in L. Trotsky, 'The Soviet Economy in Danger' (1932), in L. Trotsky, *Towards Socialism or Capitalism?*, London: New Park Publications, 1976, p. 100.
42. M. Lewin, 'The Disappearance of Planning in the Plan', *Slavic Review*, vol. 32, no. 2, June 1973, p. 276.
43. See Cohen's introduction to the revised edition of his biography of Bukharin.
44. M. Lewin, *Political Undercurrents*, p. xii.
45. S.H. Cohen, *Economic Development in the Soviet Union*, Lexington, Mass.: D.C. Heath, 1970, p. 70.
46. See H. Hunter, 'The Overambitious First Soviet Five-Year Plan', *Slavic Review*, vol. 32, no. 2, June 1973.
47. N.I. Bukharin, 'L'organisation de la force armie et la structure de la société', *Bulletin Communiste*, vol. 1, no. 7, 24 April 1920, pp. 7-8.
48. E.H. Carr, *Foundations of a Planned Economy 1926-1929*, vol. 2, London: Macmillan, 1971, pp. 329-30.
49. The opposition is quoted in W. Korey, 'Zinoviev's Critique of Stalin's Theory of Socialism in One Country', *American Slavic and East European Review*, vol. 9, December 1950, p. 260.
50. *Pravda*, 18 August 1927.
51. R. Day, *The 'Crisis' and the 'Crash', Soviet Studies of the West (1917-1939)*, London: New Left Books, 1981, pp. 109-10.
52. Parts of the relevant speeches are translated in R. Daniels (ed.), *A Documentary History of Communism*, vol. 1, New York: Vintage, 1962, pp. 306-8.
53. Ibid., pp. 308-9, for a translation of short extracts.
54. N.I. Bukharin, 'Finance Capital in Papal Robes', *Inprecor*, vol. x, no. 14, 20 March 1930, pp. 246-7.
55. Cohen, *op. cit.*, p. xv.
56. A. Solzhenitsyn, *The Gulag Archipelago*, vol. 1, London: Collins, 1973, p. 413. See also R. Medvedev, *Nikolai Bukharin. The Last Years*, New York: Norton, 1980.
57. Text in R. Medvedev, *Let History Judge*, London: Macmillan, 1972, pp. 182-4 (my emphasis).
58. N.I. Bukharin, 'Nekotorye problemy sovremmenogo kapitalizma u teoretikov burzhuazii', and 'Teoriya "organizovannoi bezkhozaistvennosti"', reprinted in *"Organizovannyi kapitalizm"*, Moscow: Communist Academy, 1930, pp. 169-99. The latter is translated as 'The Theory of "Organised Economic Disorder"', in N.I. Bukharin, *Selected Writings on the State, op. cit.*

59. Day, *op. cit.*, p. 170.
60. 'The Theory of "Organised Economic Disorder" ', *op. cit.*, pp. 350-1.
61. *Inprecor*, vol. x, no. 54, 27 November 1930, p. 1120.
62. Ibid.
63. Katkov, *op. cit.*
64. Cohen, *op. cit.*, p. 352.
65. N.I. Bukharin, 'Marx's Teaching and its Historical Importance', in N.I. Bukharin *et al.*, *Marxism and Modern Thought*, London: Routledge, 1936, p. 80.

7   COMPLETING THE SYSTEM

During August and September of 1929 Bukharin and his theories were hounded in the Soviet press. Triumphant Stalinism grew on what Barrington Moore Jr has called 'the mortality of ideas' and the complex of ideas that made up Bukharin's analysis of capitalism and the transition to socialism was one of the first to go under. While this witch-hunt was going on, the American economy had begun to turn down almost unnoticed by contemporaries. Then, in October 1929, the New York Stock Market crashed and it became clear that the 'temporary stabilisation' of capitalism was over although the full magnitude of the depression was slow to be realised as the world economy lurched downwards over the next three years. Bukharin had never suggested that the tendencies towards state capitalism that he claimed to have identified in the West had gone so far as to eliminate the crisis mechanism in capitalism. He had only considered this possibility, as we saw in Chapter 3, when he explored the model of 'pure' state capitalism. So far as the capitalism that he saw around him was concerned, he had emphasised the complexity of crisis-inducing factors over single-cause theories. Nevertheless, in the first instance the extent and generality of the crisis seemingly 'tore the ground from under Bukharin's feet'.[1]

But the situation soon proved more complex than this. The depression was no simple return to the nineteenth-century crisis-cycle, and it involved only a temporary retreat from the state capitalist trends from 'above' and 'below' that Bukharin had seen in the 1920s. Within a short time both trends were reappearing in an intensified form. In this sense the events of the first world war and the 1920s created what some historians have seen as analogues for the solution to later problems of capitalism. In these terms capitalism in the 1920s was in a transitional era where, as the American historian Charles Maier notes, one finds the 'darkening twilight of the liberal era. But if a twilight decade, the 1920s was also one of morning as well as dusk, slowly bringing into focus the transformations that carried capitalist societies through a half-century of transit.'[2] By the time of Bukharin's death in 1938 the nature of this new morning was becoming apparent, showing that Bukharin had not been wrong when he had argued that 'the future belongs to forms close to state capitalism'.

By 1938 in Russia the economy had been driven forwards at a

relentless pace. The aim of catching up with the West was a chase after a moving target constantly reinforcing the drive to push up production. Yet in the Soviet Union itself, and for the communist movement that was controlled from it, this very development of the productive forces became identified with the development of socialism. It was Stalin himself who laid down this approach in a famous passage, 'first the productive forces of society change and develop, and then, *depending on these changes and in conformity with them*, men's relations of production, their economic relations change.'[3] Stalinism as an ideology had regressed back beyond Lassalle's statism to the developmentalism of Saint-Simon. Then, in the aftermath of the second world war, the forms that had been created in Russia were extended to encompass Eastern Europe. The rhythm of the march of 'socialism' was no longer just that of the throb of machinery, it now became the tramp of Red Army boots.

But much had also changed in the West by this time. In 1938 the German economy was booming at more than full-employment levels as German capitalists were regimented at the behest of the Nazi state. This degree of subordination of private capital to the state creates insuperable difficulties for any analysis which seeks to understand the state or fascism as some agency for big business. In these terms the specific relationship that developed in Nazi Germany has been described by one leading historian who has sought to break away from this approach as *'unique in the history of modern bourgeois society and its governments; it is precisely this that must be explained.'*[4] Yet if the Nazi state is seen as an intense variety of what Bukharin had analysed as state capitalism its uniqueness seems less apparent. To a degree unparalleled elsewhere in the West the various contradictions that developed under fascism in Germany forced an ever-greater leading role on the state. But the difference was one of degree, for elsewhere too the experience of the depression of the 1930s forced a greater economic, social and military role on the state as the process of international competition intensified in the world economy.[5]

Then in the second world war, as in the first, the commanding role of the state came more to the fore, even in the 'democracies'. The talk was again of a 'war socialism' as society was subordinated to an even greater extent than it had been between 1914-1918 to the effort of total war. Everywhere the states that emerged from the other side of this experience found themselves with a larger share of activity under their control, save in the defeated fascist states. And even in these the role of the state was significantly higher than in their pre-fascist years.

Some deduced from this experience that it was war itself that was the mechanism that displaced private capital in favour of state capital. But the post-war experience has not borne this out as the ties between state and capital have been drawn tighter throughout advanced western capitalism — albeit at a slower and varied pace.

Nor is this trend confined only to these societies. Even before decolonisation extensive structures of state activity and control were in place in the colonial world. Then, with independence, as the new states struggled to match themselves against advanced capitalism they were forced to expand their powers and take over the process of accumulation to such a degree that many have overtaken the advanced West in the extent of their state capitalism.

Everywhere the dynamics of this shift lie outside any simple identification with socialism or socialist ideology. It is for this reason that attempts to identify socialism with state ownership and planning (or to put it another way, to identify capitalism with private property and the market) soon break down. While it is true that the Eastern bloc states are all clustered towards the upper end of any private-state, market-plan spectrum there are also 'capitalist' nations there to keep them company. Moreover, the range is a continuum in which one would be hard put to find any break. And where in any case should one look? Does capitalism end with 49 per cent state ownership, or is it 51 per cent, or even 75 or 80 per cent? Any figure is arbitrary. What then is to be done with state control when legal title is left nominally in private hands? Attempts to go further and to test what one commentator has called 'the socialist web hypothesis' — that the concentration of state ownership will be accompanied by such features as planning and control, high government expenditure and so on — break down equally quickly. The hypothesis shows itself to be 'quite inadequate'.[6]

But the difficulties with the conventional hypotheses (whether of the Right or the Left) are not only apparent here. The increased role of the state has nowhere meant that countries have been able to detach themselves from one another. The usual accounts cannot cope with this. Either the state is supreme, in which case 'interdependence' (to use the term of those who deal in these issues) is on the way out; or it is 'interdependence' which is supreme, in which case it is the state which is on the way out. And yet we seem to have both. 'Interdependence' should mean the breaking-down of barriers, the integration of nations, write a group of perplexed American observers, but the highest 'interdependence' 'would actually be attained by opponents in war!'[7] The problem is, of course, to deal with the dialectic of what Bukharin discussed as the tendencies towards nationalisation and internationalisation within the world economy. It is this dialectic that has been at work throughout the entire history of capitalism. At one level it has continuously tied the world closer together making any attempt to create 'islands' or 'second' or 'third' worlds of socialism ever more utopian. At another level, it has differentiated us all into supposedly separate state-bound compartments. A century ago there were some 50 states in the world. Today the figure has risen to more than 180, and each lays claims to the loyalty of its population; each is determined to defend what it portrays as its national integrity, if necessary to the last of that loyal population. In this way they remain imprisoned within the capitalist world economy because none of them has tried, nor can they try, to overturn it. When they fight against it they jockey for position, they do not attempt to pull the system down.

At the beginning of the twentieth century socialists comforted themselves over the disappointments of the late nineteenth century with the thought that the new century would be different. It has been, but in ways far more terrible than they could have imagined. Modern socialists have still not fully got to grips with this. Bukharin's analysis, we have argued, offers that possibility. Its importance cannot be derived so much from abstract discussions of Marxism and method. One can find these in Bukharin and, as with others, they create more problems than they solve. Taken as a whole Bukharin's Marxism embodies many problems. Ultimately he was led so far astray in his politics that he unwittingly contributed to one of the central horrors of this century. Sometimes, even when he was right, it was perhaps more because he had a sensuous grasp of a point than a conscious theorisation of it. But this is not how we should judge his contribution. Bukharin's importance lies in his analysis of capitalism itself and the way in which the transition from it must occur. It is on this that he stands or falls, and it is on this that we have based our estimation of his importance.

In the first place, Bukharin's conception of capitalism was not that of an abstract model, an ideal type which is held up to the world. Capitalism was not to be reduced to a simple formula whether that formula be commodity exchange, wage labour, the market, private property, or whatever. For Bukharin capitalism was a dynamic mode of production which is constantly in the process of transforming itself. What Marxists must do is to understand the nature of this constant transformation and not erect timeless categories into which an intransigent reality has to be hammered. Bukharin found the unifying element of the different forms of capitalism in the self-expansion of capital itself. It is this competitive drive of capital to expand that gives capitalism its dynamism, and it is this that works through time to alter the forms of the system. Thus capitalism as it matures and ages can overcome the forms that seemed to characterise its youth. Private property and the market are displaced in favour of state property, control and planning. Labour becomes a chained commodity. Commodity exchange itself is transformed and developed to higher levels of military competition which in our own time threaten to exterminate us all. But the drive to expand remains and it works through all these forms. Production is not controlled by man. The law of value in the sense of the anarchic social validation of labour through competition continues to impose itself on individual capitals and state capitals.

But secondly, if we are to understand this, Bukharin argued that we must focus on capitalism as a totality. This totality, he argued, lies in the world economy. It is here that capitalism receives its fullest development as from the very outset of its existence it has driven outwards. Yet the world economy too has a history. It does not exist as an abstract category which is imposed on us from outside. Just as capital develops through it so has the world economy developed through capitalism.

Here we are led, thirdly, to Bukharin's stress on the manner in which the contradictions within the world economy have worked through time to produce the hypertrophied tendencies towards state capitalism. In his youth he had read Hobbes' *Leviathan*, but in the developments of the first world war he found the prospect of a future against which Hobbes' fantasy appeared as no more than a 'a child's plaything'. Socialism would have to be the negation of this vision. It had to be based upon overcoming the capitalist state and its state capitalism, not on extending it.

In these terms, fourthly, Bukharin saw that socialism could be nothing other than the conscious subordination of society to man, and it was only the working class that could lead this. Only in this way could the dominating power of capital be overcome; that is, only through its conscious suppression. It is not a transformation that can be made over men, whether they be workers or peasants; it is a transformation that they themselves must make. It is not a transformation that can be made by proxy. But, if we look around the world at those states which claim to have broken capitalism, nowhere do we find the liberation of man. Everywhere socialism is the name that disguises the proxy whether it be the army, the bureaucracy or the Party. Bukharin retained this vision of socialism. In the end he failed not because he gave it up but because he could not look the full reality of the degeneration of the Russian Revolution in the face.

It is here that we need to extend and complete his analysis. He did go further, as we have seen, and grasp in outline the possibility of degeneration that faced all revolutions, and the Russian Revolution in particular. He saw that if revolution was a political act with which the negation of capitalism and state capitalism had to begin then so it could be reversed. But he did not see all of the pressures that would be working in that way. He failed to follow through his discussion how the pressures of the old relations of production worked against the transitional society both nationally and internationally. Against this we have insisted that if capitalism is made as a totality then it can only be broken that way. And if the totality of capitalism rests ultimately at the level of the capitalist world economy then so does the possibility of socialism rest with overcoming it there too. It is here, through an extension of Bukharin's analysis of the interaction of state and capital within the world economy, that we find the real logic and necessity for the revolution to be permanent.

Such a task is a huge one. It is far easier to delude oneself into believing that, however barbaric the forms, there already exist societies that have begun it. They have not. But a recognition of this only takes us back to the situation before 1917. Then too socialists could not point to a 'haven' where their ideas had been implemented. They could only point to the death and destruction of the capitalism that was around them and the optimism that it did not have to be this way, that man could overcome the system that had brought him to the slaughter of his fellow man.

Today the threat of destruction is greater than ever. But that optimism still exists despite all that the twentieth century has done, perhaps even because of it. If we are to take hold of it again then as a first step we must come to terms with the world as it is. It is here that Bukharin's analysis of capitalism and the transition to socialism can assist us. We have not pretended that it is complete or without problems, but we have argued that it is essential to take it up and take it forward if we are to understand the modern world: East, South and West. Here Bukharin needs no epitaph from us. He wrote his own in the introduction to his *Economics of the Transition Period*: 'The author would consider his work fulfilled if those who have begun an analogous train of thought would put it into a final form . . .'.

Notes

1. R. Day, *The 'Crisis' and the 'Crash': Soviet Studies of the West (1917-1939)*, London: New Left Books, 1981, p. 178.
2. C. Maier, *Recasting Bourgeois Europe. Stabilization in France, Germany, and Italy in the Decade after World War I*, Princeton, New Jersey: Princeton University Press, 1975, p. 594.
3. J.V. Stalin, 'Dialectical and Historical Materialism', in *History of the CPSU, Bolsheviks, Short Course*, Moscow, 1939, p. 122 (emphasis in the original).
4. T. Mason, 'The Primacy of Politics: Politics and Economics in National Socialist Germany', in S.J. Woolf (ed.), *The Nature of Fascism*, New York: Random House, 1968, p. 167 (emphasis in the original).
5. See J. Garraty, 'The New Deal, National Socialism and the Great Depression', *American Historical Review*, vol. 78, no. 4, October 1973.
6. F. Pryor, *Property and Industrial Organisation in Communist and Capitalist Nations*, Bloomington, Indiana: Indiana University Press, 1973, chapter 1.
7. R. Rosecrance *et al.*, 'Whither Interdependence?', *International Organisation*, vol. 31, no. 3, 1977, p. 426.

INDEX

For Product Safety Concerns and Information please contact our EU
representative GPSR@taylorandfrancis.com
Taylor & Francis Verlag GmbH, Kaufingerstraße 24, 80331 München, Germany